DANCE
WITHOUT
STEPS

DANCE
WITHOUT
STEPS

PAUL BENDIX

The Oliver Arts & Open Press

Library of Congress Control Number: 2011937418
ISBN: 978-0-9829878-5-8
Bendix, Paul. 1946
Dance without Steps
by Paul Bendix

Cover and book design
Alan Hunns   alan@hunnsgraphics.demon.co.uk
Cover illustration
Eva Mautner   evamautner@gmail.com
Cover picture
Getty Images

The Oliver Arts & Open Press
2578 Broadway (Suite #102)
New York, NY 10025
http://oliveropenpress.com

For Marlou

"He was, in many ways,
the best reminder of all.
That this is life, that it is a voyage,
that the essential conditions are rough,
and that it all ends."

CONTENTS

ON A ROLL

DESERT BOY

IN THE GARDEN

CONTENTS

TRAVELS

On a Roll

How to Make Pea Soup

JULY 2009

Step Number 1
Become a quadriplegic. This is difficult, but it is not impossible. See Appendix.

Step Number 2
Prepare your vegetables. Note that Trader Joe's will prepare your vegetables for you, vis-à-vis Trader Joe's Mirepoix, $2.50 cheap – but not sporting. In fact to be truly in the spirit of the endeavor, grow your own. At least your own onions and garlic. Carrots? Buy the colorful ones at the Sunday farmers market. Celery is celery.

Onions in their natural state come attached to an enormous stem, a.k.a. onion top, which makes the crop easily transportable but confuses the issue. The issue: What is edible? Are you supposed to eat the green part, like a spring onion? How springlike is an onion you buy in the summer? What about a spring onion you buy in January? If you tend to think about these things, have someone else deal with the onions for you. Chop off the tops, dispose of them in a distinctly non-compost way, and get on with it. Getting on with it is very important in making pea soup.

Growing your own garlic is fun, unless you bugger off to Europe around harvest time and return to find that the green garlic tops, pointing like a street sign to the subterranean treasure, have withered, even rotted, into nothingness. Other crops have displaced the garlic airspace... which means you will have some frantic digging to do. Never mind, for a head of garlic is unmistakable, even with dirt clods on it. In fact, all you need do is shake off the dirt and roll inside for your Garlic Preparation.

Place a head of garlic inside a small plastic bag, seal the bag and place it under your left wheelchair tire. The big tire, of course. Roll forward. There will be a crunching sound, but do not be alarmed. If you must, really must, open the bag and look inside. You will find that the first tire roll did very little but separate the cloves. Roll back and forth a few more times to actually separate the peels from the cloves... and the men from the boys. This is a gratifyingly macho activity, and it doesn't hurt to yell various things like "die you garlic fuckers" while you roll about with your wheelchair.

Empty the contents of the plastic bag onto a plate. Yes, it looks a bit chaotic, but so did early Jackson Pollock. All you have to do is separate peels from garlic. And, okay, so there's probably a little dirt in there too. There's probably a little dirt everywhere. Don't worry about it. Cleanliness is not next to godliness. Cleanliness is next to San Diego.

Once the garlic is peeled and crushed, you will feel so good about yourself that the rest of the cooking process will occur almost naturally. Carrots are foolishly designed with green tops and stringy root ends. No problem. Bite off either and with your teeth. That is correct. This is a dental process. Is anyone looking? I should hope not. Quadriplegic cooking is no one's business. What happens in the kitchen stays in the kitchen. The alternative to end-and-top carrot biting involves the use of a knife. This is to be avoided. If God had intended quadriplegics to use knives, he would have given them fingers. Which means, of course, bite not only the ends but the middle... in fact, bite as many times as necessary. If you fear the addition of saliva to your recipe, rinse the suckers off. Remember, no one need know. And if they ask, refer them to the soup. Which, I assure you, will be very good.

Celery, onions... well, here one must cede ground to the neurologically complete. Briefly, very briefly, grab a knife, stab each onion on a cutting board with nails sticking up (a standard rehabilitation kitchen device, believe it or not) to stabilize things. Then cut the onions into quarters, slipping them free of their peels. The celery... either bite or cut... it takes as long either way, the stuff being so stringy. Then move on to automation.

The Cuisinart. This is a Serious Machine. It is French. The French invented other Serious Machines, such as the guillotine.

So don't buy a wimpy little Cuisinart. Get a big mother. Throw all the vegetables described above into its maw and then: press "chop." Don't press "on," because your big macho Cuisinart will, within a couple of nanoseconds, reduce all the vegetables to subatomic particles.

Step Number 3

Meat. The trick is to worry a lot about this step. In fact, don't take a step unless it is a guilt-ridden step. Why guilt? Because you have made efforts, albeit nominal, to be something of a slightly practicing Jew. And you know, just know, that pea soup is inescapably German, and that other inescapably German thing, a.k.a. schwein, can be avoided the way scones spurn Devon cream. You need the ham hock, known in the UK as a ham knuckle, if you are to make a credible pea soup. The trick is to make the ham hock/knuckle kosher. How to do this? The technology may not yet be available, although this is not entirely clear. I believe the answer is in development and under wraps and will appear shortly. Meanwhile, in the absence of Pork Koshering Technology, one will have to settle for virtual PKT.

Step Number 4

Purists will insist that you must add peas to pea soup. Very well, have it your way. Dump in some dried peas. Okay, add some broth or something. But to be really cool, and to give the sense that you actually know how to cook – throw in some frozen peas at the last minute. Frozen peas are, you know, green and bouncy. They will make the soup feel green and bouncy. So set off for Trader Joe's with frozen peas in mind, and by the time you have bought some cooked brown rice, noted what's new in chicken burritos, seriously considered the fresh batch of Stilton and thought hard about another bottle of wine... you will have forgotten about the frozen peas and return home without them. Never mind. You didn't need them anyway.

Step Number 5

Cooking is the easiest step of all, the one that requires the least effort and absolutely no knowledge. Plug in the Crockpot. Slightly differently, plug in the slow cooker. You've heard of slow cuisine? Well this is the slowest. In fact, expect your pea soup to cook overnight. Even for a week. Don't rule out a year. And maybe for the entire Obama administration. Go slow; that is the general quadriplegic rule under any circumstances. This pertains both to cooking and to....

Step Number 6

Eat slowly. Remember, there are many little bones in the Koshered Pork, and because you have committed an obvious transgression, you can count on those bones to drift to the bottom of the cooker, leap invisibly onto your spoon–then lodge directly in your gullet. Be careful, and if you're not too stressed out, enjoy.

Slow Going

FEBRUARY 2005

I've stopped walking. Though I've been told, quite methodically, by a succession of physical therapists, that I'd better shake a leg. I'd best get up occasionally from my sedentary desk life, seize my crutch, and schlep my middle-aged butt up and down the hallway. I used to remember to do this. No, not all the time, but often enough. Usually, the incentive was urinary. You can't drink coffee and sit at a desk forever. But this habit of ambulation has died. Now I hit the joystick of my wheelchair and head from desk to bathroom to kitchen under battery power. I hadn't really noticed.

I guess I've been preoccupied. Working with a high school community – the campus, its PTA and parents and well-wishers – has finally made me feel a part of things. And the word "finally" is essential in this description. Only recently, I have realized that among the high school band boosters, black student advisors, librarians, English teachers, principals and parents, I am wanted. I belong. I contribute.

There's only one adult restroom on a two-thousand-student campus that can really take a wheelchair. The disabled parking spaces tend to be full of athletic-looking parents. I still haven't found the school's T-Wing. And people have a way of asking me, despite my paralyzed right hand, to take notes in meetings. Of course, this last request, the note-taking part, signals my inclusion. Schools are such frantically needy places, and everyone involved is so desperate for help, that even the neighborhood quadriplegic looks good. And in an atmosphere in which everyone is expected to try, the neighborhood quadriplegic fits right in. So, I'm part of something big and human. And I need them, and they need me.

I feel much the same way about the suburban downtown where I've lived for something like fifteen years. In knowing the people in the local espresso outlets, the library, the service stations and the restaurants, I have come to know myself. To believe that I give people something in being with them. This often consists of a straight look in the eyes. I've learned, in many small ways, to give people credit for being people.

Will America survive its current individualistic frenzy of Me-ism? I think so, especially on days when I go around downtown on flimsy errands, in search of companionship as much as a quart of milk and laundry detergent. Writing is a lonely business, and existence is a lonely business, but business itself isn't so lonely, so I frequent businesses. The guy in the tea shop who says his Yorkshire Gold tea bags will be in next week. The dry cleaner who screwed up my trousers. The librarian who has my Hamilton-Paterson on hold behind her counter. I need to talk to them, to acquire this and inquire about that. I need to take them in, appreciate them, and exchange something. This belief that I have something to exchange, this wasn't always there.

I must've spent the first ten years of my disabled life trying to delude myself that I wasn't disabled. I was mostly unemployed in those years, but when people asked what I did for a living, I never suggested that my newly disabled state had thrown me off stride, even in the slightest way. I was in this field, and looking for that job. I was in school. I was doing this part time, bottom-of-the-barrel work now, but never mind. I was always a professional, even when I was a professional on food stamps. In one of my early jobs, working as an outreach person for a rehabilitation hospital, I didn't even have a desk. I had a metal typing stand, and I borrowed a phone from the person in the adjoining desk. It was pretty silly, pretty dismal, and quite humiliating for someone who had a graduate degree and high hopes for himself. Life would have been much less painful in those days if I'd simply been able to say, I've had a setback and this is how things are.

I say that now, much more often, in my daily excursions into town. I don't know how I say it, but I more often believe it. I have had a setback, you have had a setback. And now I'm at a point in life in which I can set back, set a spell. And give. And take. That's the other part.

Marlou and I just traveled to Arizona. These days, when I travel anywhere, there's a setback for every advance. In Phoenix, the bedroom in my sister's house has a low futon with an upward tilt at the edges of the mattress. This is all it takes to prevent me from easily rolling over on one side and grabbing things at night. This combined with the throw rugs on the floor that grasp my paralyzed leg like aliens, the sheer distance across the living room, the toilet that seems built at child height – it all sends me into a quiet rage. In maneuvering around my sister's house, I feel like I'm walking through mercury. Progress is slow and painful. I have to remember to stand and begin moving five minutes before my bladder capacity (diminished) runs out. The ten-minute ride to my nephew's swim meet requires an additional ten minutes at either end, as I make my halting way up from the sofa, across the living room, and out the door.

Of course, with my wife and sister around, women are waiting on me hand and foot, and with both limbs paralyzed, this makes all the difference. It makes all the difference in terms of practicality, and it gives me a sense of hope. Someone cares about me and supports my tea drinking, taco eating, newspaper reading and showering. Still, I don't like being quite so dependent, especially on my wife. At home, things are set up to enable me to be quite independent. Marlou may help me on with my socks, trousers and shoes in the morning. Or, sometimes, just the socks. But if she doesn't have the time, that's okay too. I can function on my own. But not in Phoenix. In that far country, things are too different. I need help.

These days, I'm not always the last person off the airplane. All my life, I've been a good passenger, a good patient, really. Being slow, I wait till other passengers have made their way up the aisle. But these days, often seated in the front row of an airplane for shorter flights, I don't always wait for the other passengers to exit. Sometimes I stand up, stick my crutch in the aisle and make my way out the door. Invariably, people back up behind me. In these years, on the cusp of old age, I am taking my place in the world. I'm learning what may be obvious to others: that in this life, place is taken, not given. Good. The more I take mine, the more I can help others take theirs.

In the Market

FEBRUARY 2006

We had a great time in that place, I tell my sister, hoping she won't ask, "what place," but she does. And the place and its location, look and minibar contents are etched forever in my brain, but the name is not. I cannot remember the hotel. I will try for hours, but it has drained, disappeared and faded from my memory. What memory? I am pushing 60, pushing it rather too hard, it appears. For as I push it, it pushes back. And there is a little too much familiar stuff, too many things recently seen, done and noted that elude recollection. Older people chuckle at this sort of thing. Memory loss is the gentlest of the many torments of aging, I believe. Much harsher to lose one's sight, give up the ability to drive, grow deaf, cease walking or find workings of one's alimentary canal on public display. No, forgetting the name of a weekend hotel is not the worst of matters. But it does suggest the rest.

Not that the rest isn't already here. Take my iPod. No, don't take it, for I love it, I use it. It has become my constant companion. But we have a rather shallow relationship, the iPod and I. As devices go, its design is utter simplicity, a matter of sliding and twiddling a single control. Nor are there terribly complex feats to accomplish. The iPod is either on or it is off. It is either playing something or not. And one either downloads a podcast or one doesn't. And when one doesn't, and one can't seem to learn how, and one purchases a book called *iPod for Dummies* without reading it, because the thing still seems too complicated, one has to ask very seriously if one isn't possibly getting older.

The whole matter takes on another dimension for someone in a wheelchair. On Sunday mornings, suburban Menlo Park is the scene of an outdoor market, a block-long procession of lettuce vendors, flower hawkers, olive oil purveyors, citrus baggers, and so on. I have a way of rolling my wheelchair up and down the stalls, eyeing this, occasionally buying that. I like the idea. The outdoor market is, after all, the quintessential village experience. People gather there not just to transact, but to exchange... the pleasantries, updates, observations and greetings that weave the social fabric. I often run into someone I know. And this reassures me, makes me feel that even without children and immediate family at hand, I have a place in some assemblage of humans. My home. My town. My market.

Menlo Park historically was a mature community. In the Bay Area, at one point it had the oldest average age per capita. It was, simply put, a senior city. Silicon Valley seemed to change all that. Menlo Park became an executive city. Children wandered the sidewalks, mothers flocked to supermarkets, everyone started to jog and restaurant cafés flourished in all weather. With the collapse of Silicon Valley, and the passage of more than five years, the town has begun to age once again. During the winter, the al fresco cafés either roll their tables inside or roll their propane heaters outside. There are not so many stroller traffic jams on the sidewalks. And the Sunday morning market is all ablaze with gray hair. And since I fit right in, in terms of age, there's no easy, simple reason for what happens to me here on a regular basis.

Would I like a pound of mushrooms? A man with a straw hat and scraggly beard displays a plastic bag a full of the very shiitakes we discussed moments ago. That will cost you two dollars, he says. We both know the mushrooms cost four dollars. Which explains why I have extracted four one-dollar bills from my wallet and now have them sitting on my lap, right next to the glowing wheelchair battery indicator. Thank you, I say, sheepishly. I hit the joystick and roll off. I'm embarrassed. The man is doing something very nice, or thinks he is doing something very nice, and with customers crowded around his stall, I don't want to point out the fifty-percent discrepancy. He is giving me a break. A price break, one that I have not sought and do not need. I'm certain this has to do with my being in a wheelchair. I am Menlo Park's Tiny Tim. I buy my lettuce, mutter God bless us every one, and make my neuromuscular way to the next stall. The lettuce lady has just given me an unannounced and unexpected free pound of French carrots. I thank her profusely. I do not know what is French about them, and I would not even know they were carrots if she hadn't insisted that the elongated yellow, rather than orange, roots were something very special. I am very special, that is what she is telling me with her free pound of vegetables. God bless us every one.

Because everyone else in the market is old, or relatively old, I cannot attribute my special status to age. And, frankly, I wonder if a younger person in a wheelchair would roll home with five free grapefruit, along with his tangerines. I am old and crippled. Aging and rolling. Hell-bent and wheelchair-bound. And somehow it is this combination that has made me the town's paralytic mascot. I don't understand it, but I don't wholly reject it. My status is as unwanted as it is inevitable. It has arrived like age itself. A very mixed bag. But thank God for the mixture.

Neither disability nor age amounts to an unalloyed curse. There are unexpected surprises. So, sir, enjoy the rutabagas. And won't you have these Chinese radishes on us?

Give an Inch

FEBRUARY 2006

We met where disabled people tend to meet, at the elevator. Both of us had just stepped off the same subway train, having reached the end of the line, the Millbrae line, of the Bay Area Rapid Transit system. A beautiful day, unaccountably sunny, the sort of day that buoys one's optimism after short cold days and long expensive nights. Our latest utility bill topped two hundred dollars for the month of February. But never mind that, and where was I? Oh, Millbrae, at the BART station. I was waiting for the elevator with a woman who wore a beautiful paisley turban, and an attractive dress covering a rather large body. With her attire and her regal bearing, she cut quite a figure, a sort of middle-aged African American queen. We made small talk. Both of us were changing to the suburban trains. She was headed for Stanford Hospital. And, gosh, she sure did hurt today. I said nothing. The elevator doors opened. We chatted about the vagaries of ground transportation in Palo Alto. She recommended the shuttle buses that frequently run between the suburban train station and the Stanford Hospital. Gosh, she said, holding her hip, but she sure did hurt today.

Because I am in a wheelchair, something excuses me from an automatic response to such a remark. I decide to exempt myself, because I had a mother who was inclined to oy vey about her life. Gave me the feeling that I was more or less responsible for her many sadnesses. So, I've been there, and I've done that, and it's unfortunate that this woman has her aches and pains, but so do I. We make our way together to the Caltrain elevator, and descend to the southbound platform. It's sunny there, too. She sits on the bench, and the man beside her says he is on his way home from Thailand. The Millbrae station serves San Francisco International Airport. The man adds that it's too bad about his pension. United Airlines is in bankruptcy and slithering out of its retirement obligations.

Hmmph, says the woman. I don't see the problem, she adds. A person's been working for decades, they've got time to get their house in order. No handouts, she says. I stare northward up the tracks. What is this country coming to? A person's employment includes a certain compensation, one part of which is the pension plan. It's not a giveaway, not a gift, and nothing remotely like welfare. But this woman has a Calvinist bug up her ass, and she is insistent. People shouldn't have their hands out all the time. People should take care of themselves. God bless America.

When the train arrives, I roll my wheelchair onto the disabled access icon painted on the floor. I smile at her. This is our goodbye and, nutty or not, she deserves some mild attention. We all do. "This is where I'm supposed to be," I tell her. "More visible to the conductor, I suppose."

"We'll see," she says.

The train rumbles in, dust flying, brakes screeching. The woman slowly gets to her feet. She is ponderous, and she walks bent over with a cane. Soon she is pointing the cane, shaking it at a young conductor, who is also black. She is telling him that the train is not in position. She wants to use the wheelchair lift. And the car with the wheelchair lift is a considerable distance away. She has been waiting, as I have, by the blue wheelchair logo on the platform. She waits here, the door opens there, and there's only one solution. The train will have to pull up.

I chortle. At first, the conductor does too. This woman thinks the train is like a bus. It isn't. For the train to "pull up," all the doors have to close, and the conductor has to have a radio conversation with the engineer in the cab.

"Are you crazy?" The conductor stares at her, and she stares at him. Two black people, the approximate ages of mother and son. Neither has to worry about being politically correct. Both let fly.

She tells him that she doesn't want any attitude. He can just put his attitude away. She wants the train to pull up, to stop where she is on the platform, open its doors and lower its lift.

The conductor tells her to wait for the next train, if she doesn't like this one. She tells him that she's never heard anyone so rude. He rolls his eyes. She waddles to the disabled car, the lift descends, and she ascends like a deus ex machina. The conductor is still muttering about her halfway to Menlo Park. She is still glaring at him. Neither will give an inch. Neither has to.

On the Street

OCTOBER 2009

The day begins, as all do, with encouragement from Cindy. "Go, Guys," says her e-mail title, the message announcing a special deal on Viagra. Cindy's friend Chrissy had gotten in touch only hours earlier concerning a male supplement, also heavily discounted, which promised to restore vigor to my life and a woman to my bed. The latter promise was somewhat vague. Never mind, for the e-mail punctuation was the message, a shower of asterisks and exclamation points, all having tremendous fun together. And if I hadn't gotten a similar note from Charles, only a few hours before Chrissy's, I might have dismissed the whole thing. But once I'd heard from Chuck, the pattern was clear. He was concerned about the actual size of my equipment. Whereas Chrissy and Cindy were focused on my efficiency. As a team approach, it all made perfect sense. Size the system to the project, target performance standards and proceed.

When I get home from this morning's errands, I will invite Chrissy, Cindy, and, why not, Charles, over for consultation. My responding e-mail will be all ***** and !!!!!!!! like theirs. And once the three of them troop into my living room, I will give everyone a glass of sparkling apple juice, crank up the TiVo and replay PBS' remarkably static *Das Rheingold*, demonstrating both the high resolution and high volume of my home electronics. A little Super Glue on the sofa cushions should keep Charles-Cindy-Chrissy's buttocks in place throughout the ensuing four hours. As for me, I will be heading for Peet's as soon as James Levine raises his baton. Should any of the three audience members protest, my response could not be clearer: ****** and !!!!!!! and thanks for sharing, and pipe down about having your butts glued to the sofa or I'm going to put the Rhinemaidens' entrance on auto-replay.

When you're retired and headed up Santa Cruz Ave., Menlo Park's main street, it is natural to review the morning's events. In which e-mails figured prominently. Not that you don't have a purpose. There is a cash machine at one end of the street. There is a pharmacist at the other. To make the acquisition of cash and the purchase of toothpaste into a major outing, you will want to stretch things a bit. Bypass the pharmacist on the first go and head directly for the cash machine. On the second pass, eastbound, pull in at the Walgreens and rummage about the dental products.

The thing is to keep up a certain pace. You don't want to appear aimless, purposeless or shiftless. Leave that to the homeless guy with the vaguely worded cardboard sign. No, you are the man with the mission. The homeless guy is from a mission. The fact that his mission is more focused and disciplined than yours... well, don't let that confuse you. Look like you know what you're doing as you proceed up the avenue. This means, don't peer around as though curious at the nature and purpose of your fellow pedestrians. After all, the townspeople vaguely recognize you. There's no passing for a tourist, so it's useless to carry a map or guidebook. It's even useless to pretend to look in the shop windows. You cannot give a credible imitation of a shopper. You do not like to shop. In particular, you do not like to shop for Persian carpets, which comprise ninety percent of what is on sale in downtown Menlo Park.

Why the need to fit in? In particular, why the need to appear productive? Or at least, not look indolent? Hard to say, but I'm working with this. There it is again, that "working" bit. Why not just tell people that I'm floating, living off the fat of the suburban land? Not even grieving. Just getting up, getting dressed and getting out... for absolutely no reason. Which would find me among the old people... and one is no longer sure who they are... anyway, the old people who stand in front of the nut display at Walgreens drugstore just a little too long.

Outed. These people are guilty of not having a paycheck or a cubicle or a commuter ticket. Unfortunately, most of these people staring at the goods in Walgreens are not Jewish, so they do not feel the guilt. They stare at the peanuts, mentally comparing the equivalent at Safeway or even trying to remember what peanuts are and what it meant when goods and services were said to cost peanuts. It's stunning to consider that the value of the nuts has risen, even as the value of the metaphor has fallen. For if things are no longer priced in peanuts, or in salt, what are they worth? Are they worth their weight in silicon? And who polishes the floors at Walgreens to such a high gloss? If I came here at night would I see some person having a go with an electric buffer? And would the rotary motion of brushes upon floor raise more questions? Better continue up the street.

What would be so horrible about being classed with George, the homeless guy who sits outside of Peet's being black, casually opening the door and holding up a sign that says Thanks for Your Help? He has signed the sign "Gorgeous George," betraying his age. I grew up near a chicken ranch owned and operated by the then-retired Gorgeous George, a forgotten wrestler. Never mind. What if it was understood that although I did not solicit public funding in quite the same way, George and I moved at approximately the same pace? In fact, by dint of door opening, many would regard George as more productive. And so what? What Puritan ethic or Calvinist belief has gotten me so paranoid?

And viewed from a more positive perspective, there is something I see in the eyes of the occasional street musician, George and a few other itinerants. An openness. They have, in the 1960s sense, dropped out and found a comfortable place in the shallows. They seem relaxed. In the present. Not forgotten. They are not out of sight... an expression that in my late adolescence signaled the ultimate or finest.

At her finest, I thought Marlou was out of sight. And then she was dying and in her most crushingly sad final days was out of sight in one eye, then the other, her brain tumors doing something ghastly to the optic nerves. And now she is gone and not out of my sight, not for long. And it all fits together, this fear of dropping out of sight, of not being seen. Which if one obsesses too mightily, distracts from seeing. Who knows what people see when they see me in my new phase of life, making my wheelchair way through the town? But it's worth knowing why I care, or what I see in being seen.

Riding Alone

NOVEMBER 2006

The thing about the commuter train to San Francisco is that it involves an ascent. Not only is one going up the map, as well as up the food chain in terms of urban life, but there is literally a step up, in fact ten or so, from platform to seating level. For wheelchairs, this is accomplished via mechanical lift. And it's that overall sense of up and at 'em, up and away, that gives these trips to the provincial capital an added boost. Of course, when the conductor announces that there is already another wheelchair on board, the experience becomes a bit less exclusive. Two of us will have special needs, be special people, take the special trip. We will have to share. No matter. One soon adjusts. Though, when the conductor adds that the other wheelchair passenger is going all the way up the Peninsula, passing stop after stop, to hit the big time, the City, I have to admit that's another matter. It's nice having the wheelchair space all to oneself. One never knows about disabled people.

Although I instantly know all I want to about this one. That she is toothless, more exactly dentureless, makes her look old. Though later, when I get a closer look, I know she is only in her late thirties, early forties. The mechanical wheelchair lift scoops me up like a shovel, swoops me into the car. I and my lead batteries blast through the open vestibule doors into the car. Hello, she says, that's a nice wheelchair. This is the moment when I take in the toothlessness, the excessive willingness to talk, the banal, and inaccurate, reference to my wheelchair. Mine, it turns out, is both smaller and older than hers. In fact, her wheelchair is new, still shiny with metallic paint, and of different design, with a broad sculpted front and a wide chassis. You going to San Francisco, she asks?

I say nothing about the wheelchair and mutter yes, San Francisco. I am suspicious of this woman, already convinced that she is a talker. Whereas, this morning, I am a reader. The San Francisco Chronicle, a folded version, sits and awaits my attention. Eric Newby's account of the Hindu Kush, with a hundred or so pages to go, also sits on my lap. This woman's account of anything can hardly compete.

Can I do anything? She directs this at me as the train picks up speed and I pick up my leg, the paralyzed one with the plastic brace, holding it by my cuff. No, I tell her. I don't need help, I don't want to interact with her; I want my foot in place and my morning unfolding as it should. That's a nice wheelchair, she says over the rail noise. She is forced to speak these words at my back, for both of us are facing forward, me in front. From my position, I can wedge my paralyzed leg against a carpeted bulkhead, keeping the foot aloft and, with it, my spirits. For once the foot has been perched, it does not need to be tended. No worries about blood clots forming, tissues swelling. The foot takes care of itself, the train takes care of itself, the trip takes care of itself. And before you know it, journalists' impressions absorbed and behind me, the Peninsula behind me, we are in San Francisco. While this woman wonders aloud if she can do anything... to help.

Being able to do anything... that's what disability is all about.

And that's why I'm painfully aware of giving this woman the cold shoulder. It can't hurt to engage her in a bit of chitchat. Just enough of an exchange to let her know, and me know, that we are not alone. Both of us require wheelchairs, wheelchair lifts to get aboard trains. And both of us take up space. We are a losing proposition for this and any other train. Our two wheelchairs occupy a disabled space that could easily hold eight chairs. That's eight full-revenue passengers, instead of two passengers traveling at a fifty percent disabled discount. We represent, both of us, an eighty-seven and one-half percent loss, if my math is right. Which it may not be, for I am both crippled and aging. I probably have twenty years on this woman. Who, incredibly, is now offering to help me pick up the Chronicle business section, which has slipped from my one-handed reading, to the floor. No thanks, I tell her. Not that the help wouldn't be welcome, for leaning hard to the left to retrieve things is one of my more frequent, and least favorite, pastimes. Anyway, she is in no position to help. Her wide-track wheelchair seems barely maneuverable. And for her to retrieve the paper, I will have to roll out of my position and into the aisle. Which simply isn't worth it. Although I can tell this would be worth it to her. She craves attention, acknowledgment. And why is her offer of help annoying? Because with Marlou ill, I need more help than ever. And pallid offers of assistance feel like a mockery. No, thank you, I tell her.

It's quite remarkable how Newby and his austere foreign-service travel companion get by on foot in 1950s northeastern Afghanistan. With each page, their achievement seems more remarkable. They are traveling up gorges that have never seen a white man, ever. Fat-tailed Himalayan sheep nearly knock them off the foot-wide paths into turning, glacier-fed rivers. While all I have to do is sit here, foot in the air, while Caltrain slows for Millbrae. Excuse me. I ignore her first sally. Excuse me. I turn my head sideways. Yes? You're going to have to move your wheelchair to one side so I can get out, she says. I nod. Excuse me... you're going to have to move your wheelchair....

We are twenty minutes away from San Francisco, I say over

my shoulder. You don't have to yell, she says. This sobers me. Was I yelling? I was certainly annoyed. And the yelling half shames me and half intrigues me. For these days, with no things trivial and everything laden with mortality, stuff is coming out. Stuff like my annoyance.

San Francisco is twenty minutes away, and moving my wheelchair to one side can be effected with the flick of a joystick. Surely she knows this, or should. No matter, for she wants to discuss it. And I want to discuss nothing with her. Now I can hear her on a cell phone. It's Mama, she tells someone. I need my medicine, she says. I need it when I see the doctor. Okay, she's heading to San Francisco to see about her health. And poor health leads to poor teeth, then no teeth, and being poor leads to all of these. And what's wrong with being poor? Nothing, except that it's scary. Almost as scary as being powerless, and disabled people are often both. Like this woman, stuck in a wheelchair, stuck with her children and her no teeth and people who won't talk to her. Uncharitable people like me.

At the San Francisco station, the conductor announces that he's going to get the two wheelchairs off the train first. Can you get by, I ask, as the woman kicks her chair into action. I'm not used to driving one of these, she says. I understand. She's new to all this. Are you getting on the Muni, she asks, referring to the city buses? I tell her yes, but maybe no. For, I guess, I am frightened to get too close to her poverty. For impoverishment as always seemed as close to me as the pavement under my wheelchair. Disabled life is lived close to the ground. Yes, but maybe no, that's what I tell her, because I want her to be on her way without me. There's something querulous about her. And people who complain about their burden and make it their lives... this possibility seems very tangible to me these days. Which is why these days I ride the Muni alone.

Nerve

SEPTEMBER 2007

If the typical middle-aged person stands before his bathroom mirror in the morning, wondering what it all means or how much longer it will all go on or what the "it" is that might or might not go on, I am atypical. My question is: Why is it all moving? And can I catch it, before it falls?

I have the unwavering sense that things are wavering. Letting go of the edge of the bathroom sink to reach for a toothbrush seems increasingly unwise. The wiser course would be to not brush my teeth. Or maybe screw the toothbrush (through that hole in the handle) to the drywall, then rub my teeth against it, like a steer at a salt lick. The other alternative would be to acknowledge that my balance is heading for that big neuromuscular museum in the sky. For me at age sixty, walking is becoming perilous. As my Dr. Wu, practitioner of Western physical medicine and Eastern hard laughter, puts it, "don't have a fall."

Instead, I have a fright each morning and several times a day. My usual stance before the sink is not stolid. It slips this way, teeters that. I can't keep my torso vertical. Bending close to the sink while brushing my teeth approaches disastrous. Especially in this hunched over posture, my center of gravity seems to drift. Worse, I don't watch my form in the mirror, don't see the way I'm leaning, getting close to tilting, then dropping. Don't have a fall.

I've had a certain amount of practical advice. My physical therapy assistant tells me, flat out, that if you don't walk enough, your balance goes. I don't walk enough. It's easy to sit in the wheelchair, get up and sit in an exercise machine, sit back in the wheelchair – a day of postural changes, aerobic exercise, and no balancing. Caroline, my cousin the doctor, tells me that a tilting neck – like mine, a cervical Tower of Pisa – can throw anyone badly off balance. So, there's that too.

One can't avoid walking, of course. My dentist, her office still decorated with floor-to-ceiling nature wallpaper dating from the 1970s, runs a strictly walk-in establishment. Railings on both sides of the steps. Wheelchair parked on the sidewalk. I enter with my crutch, clicking my way a short route from reception desk to treatment room. The journey is getting longer and longer. There seems to be nothing to the right.

Things should be on the right. It's on the right side that my body is paralyzed. It's here, with a right arm as agile as a two-by-four, that I will hit if I fall the wrong way. Toward the right is the wrong way. In a world divided into left and right, the chances of toppling rightwards hover around fifty percent. That's the way I see it. And I see it all the time. For example, taking those tentative baby steps, crutch, lurch, crutch, lurch, from my dentist's waiting room, past the reception counter, and into the no-wall and nothing-to-grab open area between dental chambers, I take it slow.

On the way out, I take it even slower. I pause at the counter to pay my bill. But there's no bill to be paid, thanks to God and dental insurance. There is a counter to lean against, but the same phenomenon occurs here. The same bathroom-sink-tilting thing. I stand and make a new appointment. I'm relieved when the receptionist accompanies me to the front door. Grabbing her arm wouldn't seem out of place. Except, I'm not there yet.

I decide that I've missed the 11:37 a.m. train home through force of destiny. There is a Safeway across the street from the station. It is a land of sparkling linoleum, crisp fluorescent lights and sanitary food dreams. The country Italian sandwich on focaccia bread is such a dream. Because it is a $4.99 dream, I take it and head for my train. The first seat is empty, the one marked reserved for the handicapped. The second wheelchair space is full, occupied by a very burly guy with a half empty pant leg. The war? Diabetes? You don't just ask people what happened to their leg. The question implies that they have been careless with limb attachment, forgetting their own need to reach and ambulate. Still, I climb out on a limb, now and then, when I sense a disabled person is open to discussion.

This guy wasn't. Hi, I said. He said nothing, just nodded that I should occupy the wheelchair space in front of him.

The problem was that the space in front of him was far from the seat behind him. I wanted a quick hobble from wheelchair to seat. Then a fast seat-to-wheelchair hobble as we rolled into Menlo Park. It seemed reasonable to ask the guy to move. Except he was as chatty as Darth Vader. I saw a simpler, easier course. Stand, walk around him, and hope the train didn't start moving. My crutch, locked to the back of my wheelchair, would take too long to remove.

I got to the seat, braced my leg against the carpeted wall, dozed and drifted through my midday retired-person's slow ride home. The 12:07 stops at every tree on the Peninsula. Still, soon it was Belmont, then San Carlos. Just to be on the safe side, I stood and made my way forward while the train paused at San Carlos Station. But not long enough. I was holding onto the seat back to my left, thinking hard about the gripless window and the too-low railing, the latter mounted at wheelchair height. The train began moving. Never mind about too low. I crouched and grabbed. Awkward, but doable.

Whispering from conductors in the vestibule. Snatches of "if he falls" and "trying to walk." Downright discouraging, this sort of observation. Also infuriating. The train was picking up speed, a faint tilt here, small jerk there. Still standing, I put my hand on the wheelchair control, felt its steadiness, let it give me neuromuscular strength. That's how things are these days. Feeling something solid either orients me in space or gives me the illusion of being oriented in space. Hard to tell. Enough to give me the courage to take one last unsupported step closer to the chair, swivel and plop into the seat.

I assured the conductor that I wouldn't fall on her shift. These train conductor women are a particularly hardy breed, two-fisted gals who hustle people on and off with a certain air, casual and firm. I wanted to tell her that we were brother and sister, all in favor of hustling, all in favor of firmness.

Back in my apartment, it was time for the crutch. Marlou wasn't home, so in case I fell.... What's the worst that could happen, I asked myself. I would fall and lie on the floor. I would fall and break my neck a second time, further damaging my spinal cord, and lie on the floor. So what? So, okay. I crutched toward the bedroom to take a nap. Then I remembered that I'd left the keys in the front door. Walk there, too? Yep. That's how the West was won. Thirsty? I crutched to the kitchen for water, conscious all the time that the vast emptiness to my right was sitting there – but I wasn't sitting anywhere. I was moving, and sometimes that's the best anyone can do.

Dentistry

AUGUST 2007

There's a difference between freeway demolition and dental work, but it's subtle and elusive. I realized this near the end of a recent procedure. Seated, that is, reclining, in a dental chair, I was experiencing the grinding and reducing of an afflicted tooth. This was the last stage before receiving a crown. No, not by way of coronation. But ending my long period of dental virginity. I have not had a cavity in thirty-five years. The only dental event of significance involved the loss of my wisdom teeth, more than twenty years ago. It's all been smooth sailing, teethwise. A cleaning here, an X-ray there, another cleaning. Another year. Another decade.

In fact, my dental seas have been as calm as the mariners' fabled doldrums. Nothing happening and nothing expected to happen.

"How did this happen?" I asked Dr. Savio. She has been my dentist from graduate school through my first marriage and into my second marriage. Our relationship, Dr. Savio's and mine, has been among the most stable in my life.

"Anything you do," Dr. Savio said, "can break a tooth. Take your pick."

I can't recall how I took my pick, thirty-five years ago. I had moved into the Noe Valley section of San Francisco because I was wanted. Wanted by a landlord who was willing to rent his studio apartment for a couple of hundred dollars a month, wanted by San Francisco State University, and maybe even wanted by the blond and amusing law student next door. She turned out to be my friend. Noe Valley turned out to be my neighborhood. And Dr. Savio, four blocks up the main street, turned out to be my dentist.

In those days, I made my way many places via crutch. It took less than fifteen minutes to hobble the few blocks to Dr. Savio's office, and what the hell, my physical therapist would have said that I needed the exercise. Besides, driving would have meant losing my parking space, the one occupied by my 1968 Plymouth Valiant. As I told my fellow English grad students, mangling Shakespeare, the valiant never taste of death but once. Nor the Dart, made by Dodge. Gas was cheap in those days. Engine viability was everything.

Dental viability wasn't a bad thing either. Visiting my father in Southern California in 1973, I'd seen a local dentist. He'd advised me that I had numerous cavities and set about filling them, which required a series of appointments. Grad school interrupted the process, and with my mouth half done I promised that dentist to finish the job up north. He seemed uneasy. No wonder. Dr. Savio poked around my mouth and said, with the lightest of airs, you don't have any cavities. I told her about the other dentist. She smiled and blinked.

Thus, thirty-five years of pain-free dentistry, and, in fact, dentistry-free dentistry. What happens in thirty-five years? Well, it can be summed up in the last appointment, the one that prepared me for the crown. First, my dental anxiety level has remained remarkably unchanged. Second, we have gotten to know each other, Dr. Savio and I, at least beyond the superficial level of pleasantries. From the 1990s, we discussed politics, speculating on why Newt Gingrich might be named after an amphibian. We talked travel. I got to know the rest of the team. The departing dental hygienist told me to be sure to visit him in retirement. Linda, who works in the front office, talked about her growing boy. On my last visit I thought of asking Linda about him. But I thought better of this, having lost track of time, and fearing that by now the son might be a law partner somewhere. On the way out, Linda asked why it was taking me so long to get from the treatment room to the front desk. She laughed, I laughed. Everyone is past treating my disability with kid gloves. The whole thing feels like family.

Of course, at the heart of it all are my teeth. My fears of dentistry have not abated. *Marathon Man*, the 1970s thriller about the evil Nazi dentist, probably has much to do with this. On the other hand, I've displayed a certain dental indomitability. Even when things neuromuscular were heading downhill, there were always my teeth. Uneventful, due for a cleaning, cavity free year after year. I can't help thinking of Walli Bendix. My grandmother, born in the 1880s, was Germany's first woman dentist. Being the first woman anything wasn't particularly cool in those days, and being the first woman Jewish anything must have made matters worse. She couldn't practice, she told me. Or did she tell Uncle Bob, her dentist son-in-law in upstate New York? It doesn't matter. Walli became a children's dentist, no adult patients allowed. She outlived my father, dying in her early nineties. I am sure she had all, or most, of her own teeth. I'm not sure how or why, but Dr. Savio would understand.

Sky Nails

FEBRUARY 2007

Marlou has had it with my fingernails. She eyes them regularly, remarking that they are something out of *L'Enfant Sauvage*. Needless to say, this is a sore point. The amount of time I devote to considering my nails and their condition can be reckoned in the nanoseconds. In fact, with Marlou occupied with the work of cancer recovery, I am surprised that she has any neurons to spare on this trivial matter. Yes, there was a time when she clipped my quadriplegic nails, regarding them like a zookeeper tending to the claws of an untidy marsupial. The curved fingers of my paralyzed right hand collide with the physical world at odd angles, routinely splitting, chipping and roughing the nails. When they grow too long, I sometimes have a go at them with nail scissors – there's a way to work around the paralysis. This is a colossal waste of time, and the strategic use of teeth makes so much more sense, my jaw being neurologically intact. Either way, the results aren't pretty or smooth.

So, one day last week, I rolled through the doorway of the solution. Sky Nails, in downtown Menlo Park. I felt that I had just crossed some sort of force field or invisible shield in entering this girls' establishment. In fact, it was only a couple of years ago that Marlou explained to me that "day spa" had nothing to do with steam baths and Jacuzzis but was, in fact, wholly devoted to nails at the ends of both extremities. All nails, all the time, all day. No night spas, apparently. So what makes it Sky Nails? Ask Rupert Murdoch what makes it Sky News. The sky's the limit. And this was my limit, somehow, enlightened though I think I am, a vague taboo probably established long ago, that this is a girls' space. Boys go elsewhere. But quadriplegics go anywhere and everywhere, sometimes landing in the world of Tupperware and ready-to-wear. Sky Nails.

Vietnam doesn't have a monopoly on fingers, but Sky Nails has cornered the market on Vietnamese fingernail servicing. The proprietor, her position evident in the tone in which she addressed the others on the staff, quietly directed me to one of the fingernail stations. I got it wrong the first time, turning my wheelchair opposite the work area. I also got it wrong the second time, trying to align the chair with the wrong side of the table. In the end, the proprietor gave up and placed a cushion on my lap. She pulled up a chair and began working over my nails. The process began with some clippers, the average, normal fingernail clippers you can buy at any drugstore. I found this rather galling. The equipment was ordinary, available only a few doors down the same street, and the clipping process took all of three minutes. I was quite prepared to pay and depart, but no, this was only the overture. Now there was filing. Okay. Everyone knows about filing, the way carpenters and metal workers give their last-minute attention to smoothing out, removing burrs, eliminating snags. The latter, according to Marlou, is what's wrong with my fingernails. They snag her. Splendid. We were at the de-snagging stage of things, fingernails appropriately sized and now attractively smoothed. Time to reach for the wallet? Forget it.

Cuticles. I can anatomically identify cuticles and do not dispute their existence. I do, however, dispute their importance. They do not concern me. They do not weigh heavily upon my soul. They do what cuticles do, acting as a buffer zone between fingers and fingernails. They require no attention, just as the white area around a printed page separates text from binding in an automatic, maintenance-free style. Don't look at your watch while Mai – as in Mai Tai – probes at your cuticles. She appears oblivious to such subtleties. She is in no hurry. There is something wrong with your cuticles, something you never considered, which is that they have grown in a natural way over your nails. Stand by. Mai will correct this defect. I stared hopelessly at her probing and shoving. I was certain there would be an end to this.

Of course, there was. But there is no end to a manicure, in the sense of objective. Well, there is, but that end is feminine in the sense of pleasurable and aesthetic. And these are dimensions I am normally attuned to, except that Sky Nails seemed a taboo women's space, and I had the acute sense of taking up too much of same. Which explains why I furtively glanced about, trying to ascertain what was happening with the three women who were undergoing various stages of fingernail and toenail work. One had tilted her head back, either dozing or in a state of Samadhi, clearly enjoying the work underway on her hands. One was talking about her toenails. The other was chatting about her work at home. Good. Maybe I wasn't in the way, disapproved of, all eyes upon me like Rosa Parks in the front of the bus.

A fourth woman entered. She was older and walked with an unusually stiff shuffle, tilting here, staggering there, a milder version of Frankenstein's gait. She settled into a chair, all smiles, even smiling at me, the unaccustomed male. She presented her hands for inspection, and one of Mai's young women turned her nails this way and that, while I started. The woman's fingers were abnormally short, abnormally straight, even bent slightly backwards like the legs of certain birds. Her hands were flaccid, muscles withered. I took this in, mentally adjusting for advanced rheumatoid arthritis. Another disabled person. My shoulder is killing me, she said to the young woman bent over her hands. There was no reaction. It was entirely possible that the manicurist did not understand. Besides, the elderly woman was staring into space now, smiling in pain. She was attractively coiffed, hair teased up like a forest of parentheses. Nicely made up, too. In short, she was pretty. She bravely forced a smile. I wondered if the manicure hurt her fingers.

I had half forgotten about Mai. By now, she was going through the wash and spin cycle. One hand was to sit in a milky bowl of water, while the other got buffed. The process reversed itself, and just when it seemed over, Mai hauled out another filing stone, followed by a polishing stone. Followed by the return of the cut-and-pick snippers. She was on a search and destroy mission, Mai was, merciless when it came to cuticle irregularities. None were to be tolerated. She kept cutting tiny nibs here, snipping miniscule bumps there. I had to give myself credit for a certain degree of bladder control.

Keep the change, I told Mai when it was all over. I didn't want the five dollars. I wanted her to have a tip, me to have a life. And now I saw that I was not an intruder. Except in the sense that the arthritic woman and I always felt like intruders, wherever we were. Our eyes met for one final moment, me displaying my warm smile of acknowledgment and it's no big deal she beaming in a way that says it's all perfectly normal and okay. Some subliminal truth passed between us, having to do with pain and shame and embarrassment, along with desperation. A sad moment, perhaps, but real as Sky Nails, real as the Mekong.

29

South Park

MAY 2008

Summertime, and the livin' isn't easy, fish jumpin' and cotton height irrelevant. In fact, it isn't even summertime, but springtime, and there is no excuse for the Fahrenheit to exceed 100 degrees. None at all.

For the spinal-cord injured, heat produces an odd effect. The respiration rises unpleasantly. One pants like a dog. Which is no sweat, which is part of the problem, for the sympathetic nervous response of sweating is largely out of action. I can blame a not-so-stray bullet for this. A neurologist would broaden this explanation. But in the end, it comes down to the same thing. It's the reason the newsletter of the Spinal Cord Injury Association advertises products such as "cooling vests." It's the reason weather in the 80s can push me over the edge. It's also the reason I get so edgy that I forget about the edge, can't even see it, in fact. Forget about it, doubt its existence.

In heat, my brain gets addled. This phenomenon is probably compounded by a certain amount of denial. In any case, it is what it is. As I grow uncomfortably hot, I become decreasingly acute. Certainly, I'm very impatient. There's probably a low level of autonomic panic going on in the background, the sense that the body is out of control. In such moments, it would be very bad of a Nigerian scam artist to ask me to send him ten thousand dollars so he can tidy up my five-million-dollar inheritance. Under such circumstances, impatience would trump practicality and common sense. Here, take my money. Just leave me alone. And turn up the fan.

In such a moment, I made a decision to finally master the TiVo in our living room. I was tired of recording, and not watching, the BBC afternoon news, and so in an inspired moment discovered that one could "select all" BBC episodes... and inadvertently erase the entire backlog of recorded programs, from opera to drama, from winter to spring, tomorrow and tomorrow. I was compos mentis enough to grasp what I had done. But not enough to absorb any messages, or care very deeply about anything but the heat. Which was rising.

The good news in such situations is that the heat-addled mind of the paralytic is largely wiped clean. Marlou's PET scan, long dreaded and much worried over by her and, of course, by me, couldn't stand the heat, as it were. So stay out of the kitchen. Go scan someone else. Like that Nigerian guy with the scoop on your inheritance. Me, I'm staring at a blank TiVo screen. Right now, life is a blank TiVo screen, only too hot and getting hotter. And fuck you, anyway, whoever you are. Just turn up the fan.

By the second disastrous day of heat, I had a plan. Such plans arise in the morning when the thermometer is still in the 70s and life has nuances and tones. San Francisco, I told Marlou. The naturally air-conditioned city. Reachable by air-conditioned train, half-hourly, and relatively empty at midday. Marlou took some persuading, after-work hours being precious, but at 1 p.m. there she was, meeting me on the northbound Caltrain platform. And forty-five minutes later, there we were, walking up blazing Fourth Street. And wondering why. Maybe it wasn't quite so hot as the South Bay suburbs, but it was hot enough. Never mind. Here was our destination, coming into view, just around the Shell gas station on Third Street. South Park.

Anyone who has spent some time in London will recognize South Park. It resembles any of the small squares that dot the British capital. There is a garden in the middle, and terraced housing on all sides. The shape of South Park is an elongated oval, straight most of the distance, rounded at the ends. By California standards, the place is authentically old. The buildings are Victorian. Gentrification has hit in a big way. South Park was a major center for dot-com companies in the last decade. Now it's home to restaurants, an upscale shop or two and loads of architects, designers and attorneys. What the hell. In the midst of the city, there's a pleasant smallness to it. Local squares in Islington, North Kensington and other

London boroughs project much the same feel.

The sidewalks at Café Centro, at the midpoint of the square, are barely wide enough for one row of outdoor tables and one passing wheelchair. But this is part of the charm. A couple of double espressos, one (that's right) shared biscotti, and we were in business. Which is to say, the business of not having any business but hanging out. Being part of café society in one of the most European bits of Western America's most European city. The breeze came up. It blew straight down the side street, Jack London Way. I gave Jack a wave. He had done well.

The woman behind us chattered on a mobile phone. The wind blew her words up the street, away from South Park, out and over the Bay. Eventually, the breeze blew her away too. Marlou and I had the place to ourselves. I stared at the oval garden, appreciating the miracle of London on no dollars a day. Marlou talked about present and future. What she has learned from her cancer experience. What mark she would like to leave in the world. The breeze had become steady, pleasantly cool. It is my natural tendency to think of what to do next. There were movies. The San Francisco Museum of Modern Art just up the street. The waterfront. The problem, as someone pointed out to me recently, is that I come from a family so disturbed, in which quiet moments of togetherness were pierced with such cruelty, that I am inclined to keep on the go. Even when there is nowhere to go and no need. It takes a discipline for me to stay put. That's why I have Marlou.

South Park was designed by George Gordon in the 1850s. Californians were still dizzy with gold fever, but Gordon came from a cooler clime. He was British. Gordon made his fortune in sugar and real estate. As for the latter, bragging inaccurately that the site south of Market Street was the only sand-free location in the city, he went to work on an ambitious project. South Park was to be the first of many such places. His scheme was to "lay out ornamental grounds and building lots on the plan of the London Squares, Ovals or Crescents." He got as far as South Park, but simple demography soon got in the way. Workers from the waterfront began traipsing through the swank little square. Housing values fell. People fled. The square became part of a South-of-Market industrial warehouse slum. The city took over the square as a public park around 1900. And then in 1906 all hell broke loose, seismically. South Park broke loose too and drifted toward modernity. Leveled in the earthquake, rebuilt shortly thereafter, it has, oddly, fulfilled Gordon's dream.

A tangled web, a crooked route, and here we are. Or there we were, hours later, our apartment still too hot for human occupancy at 8 p.m., sitting outside on our patch of lawn. No need to go anywhere. We were home. Going was over. At one point, Marlou gazed across what can only be described as our concrete parking area. She seemed to be looking at the sky. I asked what she was thinking. A song, she said, something we had learned in our chorus. An African song. Something primal. Whatever it was, just then I felt her repose, her capacity for genuine peace— the very qualities that tend to elude me in my life. Before going inside, we remarked on the strangeness of not eluding each other. That we had met. And in the heat and in the dark we were for a long lingering moment, grateful.

Desert Boy

Softening

OCTOBER 2007

From my desert home, I could see the Chocolate Mountains (named only for their color), fifty miles away. In fifteen years of living in our small town, I never ventured near the craggy range. Which was just as well. Arid, entirely mineral, the Chocolate Mountains could stay where they were. And so would I. Besides, I had much better mountains at home, with snow on the peaks most of the year. Well, much of the year. Actually, one peak was invisible from our house, for the mountain range shot up in front of it like a wall, its twelve-thousand-foot summit lost behind foothills and ridges. But the other peak sat there like Mount Fuji, conical, steep and capped with white. Once I was old enough to attend summer camp and climb the thing, Mount San Jacinto was revealed to be topped with white granite. The actual snow was twenty miles away, as the crow flies, if the crow flies with a miniature oxygen tank and has been working out at the local crow gym. That was the white streak atop Mount San Gorgonio, on the opposite side of the pass, the peak I couldn't see from my home. Visible or invisible, it didn't matter. In between these stark geological upthrusts the desert lay out, panting with heat stroke. Low, hot and hopeless. The mountains held the miracle of water. And of snow.

In between the mountain ranges, the land rose to about two thousand feet, high enough for the winter snows to gradually creep down the slopes until they reached the desert. This happened every year or so, as I recall. And I recall poorly, for what kid has a sense of years? There were annual events. Christmas and summer vacations, the Fourth of July. But who was keeping track of snow? I only recall waking up a morning here and another there and hearing nothing. The absence of sound derived from the lack of traffic, the absence of cement trucks that drove up and down the paved road by our home. The quarry had given up for the moment. The town had given up, and best of all, the school buses had given up. Which explained why I hadn't gotten up, sleeping in way past wake-up hour. You could see it before you even looked through the windows, such was the profusion of light, brilliant beneath dark gray skies. Snow.

The white had softened its way down the vast ridges, dropping a comforter over the desert flats, chaparral now subsumed in a sparkling sameness. The dirt road before our house had vanished. The desert fields dipped at the edge of our track, and the barbed-wire fence delineating the quarry's edge stood black. But aside from the roadside ditch, desert and driveway had become indistinguishable, everything united in cushiony folds of white. My father trudged across the 8 a.m. lawn, leaving egregious footprints behind him. Green peeked out where he had stepped. He had to be stopped. I was dressed in seconds, sliding past my mother and her oatmeal, and making for the side door.

My father said nothing, smiled faintly and continued his trudge. He seemed gently lost. Perhaps he was curious as to what linked the snows of his New York boyhood with this California moment. From inside, the foolishness of his snow tromping seemed obvious. But outside, I could see less cause for concern. The snow was falling, floating from the skies and filling in my father's tracks and my own. The richness of this, the luxury of walking on and grinding down the stuff as it renewed and replaced itself... it was more than one could hope for. I followed my father.

Building a snowman. Having a snowball fight. I knew about these things from previous years. More typically, the snow would melt fast, and one had to hustle the storybook world into reality. My father knew how to roll the snowman, first straight, then sideways. Three frozen globes was all it took, though we paid a terrible price. This action opened green swaths on the lawn, revealing the snowy day as something of a lie. Some years, the snow was so thin that it took minutes to amass a single snowball. Which I promptly threw at my brother, if he was around. It took him minutes to amass another snowball. The back-and-forth of this proceeded at such a pathetic pace that both of us lost interest. The solution involved driving up a road into the foothills where The Bench, a plateau a thousand feet higher, reliably offered real snow.

But not today. Today the real snow was here, on the ground, and my father was inspecting it, wearing old trousers no longer fit for his doctor's office. White had capped the fence posts around our property, filled an empty wagon on the patio, clung irregularly to the privet hedges. My father, hands clasped behind his back, made a raspy whistling sound. This signaled a contemplative lightness. It was a good sign, suggestive of pastimes and possibilities. No school. No office. I could see my mother at work in the kitchen. She had no interest in being outside on cold days. Something commanded her attention on the kitchen. Soup. I was sure she was making soup.

On the back lawn, my brother had something major under way with the family dog. Frosty, already off-white, raced in pursuit of a piece of greasewood. My brother threw this up and down the snowy lawn, the dog turning and skidding to grab the stick. I envied everything about my sibling. Somehow he had broken free enough to learn how to throw a softball, then a hardball and now this random piece of desert wood. Frosty scrambled over the snow, involuntarily skating sideways, unconcerned by the slippery disorientation. He caught the stick, returned it, and now I insisted on having a throw. My brother was littler, and it was embarrassing to make my underhand pitch in his presence. He didn't understand that my parents' marriage was coming apart, and we had important adult work to do. So I was staying close by my father. My brother was learning baseball.

Frosty caught my stick, fell, tumbled onto his back, and threw up snow like a plow. My brother laughed, my father smiled and I tried to understand. It was funny, our dog's effort in the snow. He was stumbling and confused and delighted. It was just another day. This one had dawned crunchy, white and slippery, but was otherwise as before, except for the addition of humans. Everyone was home. This was home. My father was laughing.

My brother and I weren't fighting. On the side steps leading to my parents' bedroom, my mother appeared with my sister. Susie wore a sweater and a puffy jacket, clung hesitantly to the wrought iron railing and watched. She headed down the steps, my mother behind. My father lifted her in the air. For once, I wasn't consumed with jealousy. It was such an odd day, after all. My mother stood outside in her housedress, unconcerned by the cold. She folded her arms and said that she had seen some strange things, but this.... Hang on, she said to my father. Moments later she returned with a movie camera. My father squinted into the ratcheting thing while my brother threw sticks to Frosty. The camera whirred, the snow fell, and my mother stood and beamed.

She seemed to be enjoying herself. The edge to her comments, the nervous rasp of her laughter, all had been absorbed by the white softness. Perhaps it would snow again. Something like this could happen, unplanned. It just came from the sky. Nothing was in its place. Nothing was in its mood. My parents were standing together, outside, as though they were happy together. No one was yelling, and no one was crying, and there seemed nothing but the prospect of a day like this. I could smell the scent of bubbling celery and onions from my mother's soup. We would eat it later, bowls steaming, the kitchen lit by gray light. All of us would eat together, it seemed, all five. There had been a softening.

After School

JULY 2005

In the burning season, every afternoon I would hurry home from fourth grade. When his doctor's office hours concluded, my dad would drive home, don old suit pants, and wander the empty fields, tossing matches here and there into the dry grasses. We were making a firebreak, he told me. At first he carried a rake and sometimes a hoe. By the time I was in fifth grade, he had bought a flamethrower, a pump-action device fueled by a backpack of kerosene. As the rough clumps of desert stubble erupted into flame, the two of us would stand and watch dry brown turn to orange, then to smoky black and white. My father stared into each blaze as though extracting a message, rocking back and forth on his feet, hands behind his back. He seemed unaware of my presence, absorbed in the flames and their grim secret. Watching him, I grew frightened and attentive.

"Your mother is the vilest bitch in hell," he would say, regarding the orange flickers. A moment later, his childhood sweetheart Virginia Himmelstein would appear to him in the fire. He should have married her, he would tell me. Not doing so was the worst mistake of his life. That, and becoming a doctor. It was important to keep him talking, to calm him, all part of my life-and-death work of saving our family. I also watched to make sure none of his fires went astray. Several blazes had gotten loose in the desert winds, and my father had become a generous contributor to the local volunteer fire department. At dinnertime, he stopped tossing matches, surveyed the charred patches and pronounced his fires out.

Calming my mother required more vigilance and imagination, and my younger brother and sister weren't much help. I knew when my mother was feeling good, because she talked and smoked with her friends. She would light a cigarette, immediately light another, then another. As she talked, her gestures expanded, her laugh grew wild, and three cigarettes burned parallel in her ashtray. She smoked only one and did not appear to notice the rest. But other people did, and when my mother was at her high-strung, erratic worst, I felt the eyes of the locals upon us. Even I could see that she no longer went to town dressed as a doctor's wife, but did her errands in frayed gardening shorts, blouse knotted, hair askew.

As her divorce and my adolescence approached, she seemed to dwell in a state of tears, anger and accusations at me. She drove too fast along the desert roads, flying into a rage at whatever child was closest. I was siding with my father against her, she said, our station wagon bouncing through rocks and dust. I thought of the fifty cents I could make washing her car. Did I believe she had a drinking problem, she asked? No, I said, Uncle Dave, her brother, had the drinking problem. I watched her neck arch, her face tighten in anger. I said, "Uncle Dave joined Alcoholics Unanimous." I had deliberately chosen the wrong word and was pleased to see her pound the steering wheel and laugh as greasewood and cactus flew by. It was important to convince her I was a child and did not dread the hours alone with her after school.

The League

SEPTEMBER 2005

First, join me for lunch hour at the Ramona High School cafeteria, Riverside, California, 1963. On my first day there, transferring from a tiny desert town in the middle of my junior year, I did carry a tray through the lunch-hour crowd. Clearly everyone knew everyone. I ate at a table alone, feeling the weight of the unwanted. The next day, I grabbed a sandwich from a vending machine, headed for the library and hid out there for the next year.

In the autumn I was a senior. A certain squeeze was on. It was running out, this phase of things, and now was my final chance to make friends. In February, I found my way into a clique and out of the library.

Four years later, 1967, I peered over the edge of my last university December and felt a similar pinch. At the height of the sexual revolution, I was Berkeley's only known virgin. I was twenty years old. Something had to happen.

Days brought a rampaging Berkeley vitality to Sproul Plaza. At lunch hour psychedelic bands on the brink of fame burst into amplified life, guitars thundering against the buildings. The campus crowds kept moving, a human river heading for the narrows at Sather Gate. Frisbees sailed overhead. Dogs splashed in a fountain. While my soundtrack was a secret Broadway song, "Where Is Love?" So unhip, so banal. Where is love? Does it fall from skies above? Where is she?

She's were all over, and that was the problem. So many, so scary, so strong. So abundant that one felt foolish. Take the Sexual Freedom League's card table in Sproul Plaza. Each morning on my way to classes I passed a tightly sweatered blonde sitting there behind a stack of brochures. Who was she? What degree of sexual freedom had she attained? It couldn't hurt to talk to her, pick up one of the brochures. Not this morning. Okay, this, the next morning. No, maybe not now, for tomorrow I would have more time. Okay, now. I leaned over the card table. Her breasts had the frightening power of rockets. They had been firing at me for months and now I was trying to say something, to thank her for the brochure, anything. How long, I asked, had she been a member of the Sexual Freedom League?

Oh, she said, she was paid to sit there. I took this in, nodding in the slow, hip way of things. Sure. Of course. Cool. All masking a strange embarrassment, like stumbling into the maintenance yard at Disneyland. What about the other card tables inviting passersby to aid the government's foreign enemies, become a harlequin, move back to subsistence agriculture? Were these people paid to sit there too? Berkeley, adulthood, the world... so much of it, so little time to understand. I dropped the Sexual Freedom League brochure in a trash can.

Judith

OCTOBER 2005

What was I doing there? Probably studying in the student union. In any case it was December, the dark of an evening, and when I came outside to unlock my bicycle and head home... the moment entered me. I raised my head, took it in, the wintry feel of things. The air crisp and dry. Light from the plate-glass interior of the student union casting its glow. Tiny sparkles in the asphalt of Sproul Plaza piqued into nighttime luminescence. Cold and dark and cozy. Pleasantly urban, people milling, striding, human warmth in a chilly night. And I could feel how this was cause for celebration, for something. Undoing the bike lock could wait. My room could not match this, whatever it was, the sparkling winter moment. The compulsive dashing from home to class, from this to that... I was used to it and now felt its emptiness. And the presence of something unaccustomed, new and mine, though nothing had changed. The night was full. And I did not know what to do except go to the pretzel guy's stand. Buy one of his pretzels, warm with yeast and promise. Which proved to be crunchy with salt and yellow with mustard. I ate the hot thing in the cold air. An unaccustomed moment before biking home, enjoying the doughy taste in the enclosing dark. It was like a summit, my senior year. I had gotten here okay. I was almost twenty-one. I had a claim on this evening and would pedal home in my own time. Such as now. I hiked my book bag over my shoulder.

I caught a glimpse, an absolutely positive glimpse, of that girl Judith. All svelteness, black tights and leotard top, the sexy intellectual, one hand on her hip, talking to someone in front of the Student Union. I unlocked my bike.

It wasn't as though we didn't know each other. We had both tried out for a campus political play, *Vietnam Follies*. Afterward in the hallway, her eyes warm, open and steady, I fumbled for conversation. See you around. And now I was seeing her around. I'd just unlocked my bicycle. But I could walk it, walk the bike over to her, and chat. Who knew?

Now I was doing that, me walking and the bike rolling, approaching her, the impossible. Hello. Oh, hello. She recognized me, even remembered my name. I could bolt right now, except she was laughing about not getting parts in the political play. We're not stars, she said. We're not even a sideshow at a peace rally, I said. Laughter being wonderful. Especially from a thin-faced Jewish beauty. And maybe we both had thin-faced Jewish beauty. This came to me now, the possibility of my own big-nosed handsomeness, hitting like a drug, exhilarating and preposterous. Though I was already running out of the next thing to say, running out of nerve. So, why don't we do coffee some time? And her face brightening said it all, so much that mine flushed and reddened in the darkness. Quickly tearing off scraps of paper from our notebooks, numbers exchanged. See you, see you. And that was it. I walked on, bike clicking through the darkness.

The night had electrified. Glints from the asphalt. Campus streetlights caressing. Lights that grabbed and threw you in the air like a trampoline. Higher than clowns in a circus. Preposterous, for they were just lights with a simple job. But I'd never seen this before, how someone had set them alight to buoy the evening. The light coming down, the whole effect bouncing up. As though life liked you.

Look at what had happened. Fear or not, I had walked up to woman, just like a man. And she had stood there... as though waiting for me. Pleased to look at me. Pleased to see me again. And soon. And now I was shaking, almost pounding, such was the physical force of this, and the evening all aswirl with lighted darkness which had the quality of caring. As though it really was mothering the soul, the alma mater. I began pedaling up the hill north of the campus. After all, it was night. Time to be heading back to my rented room in a house full of rented rooms. Which was inconceivable, for what would I do there? Stand in my room? The kitchen? There wasn't room in the rooms, not for this. I saw the traffic light turning green at Cedar Street and kept going. This woman had such knowing eyes. Adult eyes. Eyes that saw and let it be known that they had seen. Seen me, and seen the best of me.

My legs forced the pedals down like pistons, forcing the bike up Euclid Avenue. Equal and opposite reaction. Pedaling up into the hills, getting higher with each block. The hills did that, they took you up. And the higher you got, the more you looked down. And what was down was small in the distant individuality of each light, and manifold in the sparkling aerial weave. And somehow this was Berkeley, where despite the occasional honk from a passing car, for I wasn't paying much attention to the night traffic... the urban hillside was singing with night. By the summit, I was singing too, old songs from my parents' record player. I was surprised that I still had the songs, even though the records were gone. The night had grown much colder with altitude. My room at the bottom of the slopes would be warm. Judith would like it, with all the carpet and the windows.

Oddly cold on the bike ride downhill. It took no leg energy to coast, so the body was cooling just as the wind chill was blasting. My face stung, my balls shrank. It was a relief to finally swing one leg over the bicycle seat and stare at the brown shingles of my house. They were nailed one over the other, the shingles, always had been, and were no different now. But they stood out in the dark, their grooves, ridges and mini-shadows revealed in the streetlight. I walked my bike along the side of the house, locked it, but couldn't quite go inside, cold or not.

Dates

OCTOBER 2005

I had been worrying about this date all week, but not now. Things were in the moment, and they were happening. Geary Boulevard was happening next. Not to worry, because streets did this, some going one way to the right, others one way to the left, and there it was. The Geary Theater. An ornate old house, like the ones around Times Square. Our provincial Broadway. Such a big-city feel for a guy from a little town. An exalted setting for a first date. Of course, I couldn't afford the tickets. Which didn't matter, because we were students, and if we just stood around handing out programs for half an hour, we could see the play free. As ushers

Judith looked bewildered at distributing programs in the theater lobby. Someone told us to move apart, one to the balcony, one to the orchestra. This possibility had not occurred to me and induced a mild panic. I was doing one thing, she another, separated by long flights of stairs. How incredibly stupid. Some date. In my mind, we would be handing out programs together, chatting in between volleys of arriving theatergoers. But she was somewhere up on the balcony, probably getting disgusted, maybe even thinking of slipping away and heading home. As the crowds thinned and the curtain neared, I dashed up the stairs. She was still there. I guided her down to the orchestra and proudly grabbed two empty seats in the back. Soon the play was under way, and we were cozily seated in the dark.

I now grasped my next miscalculation. Pinter's *The Homecoming* seethed with menace and dark family undercurrents. A comfortable milieu for me, but not the cheeriest date... and why hadn't I suggested a movie and a coffee, like a normal guy? Welcome to my theater, Judith, isn't this something? Fancy, urban and grown up. Aren't we having fun with Pinter and his inexplicably menacing family? I thought of taking her hand, holding it in the dark. I thought of... almost anything but this. The house lights came up at intermission. Let's go, I said. Judith brightened. The play's not the thing. Judith was. To hell with the second act. There was a brightly lit coffee shop across the street.

Judith and I each ordered pie. She had coffee. I watched her stir in cream. Her sleepy, sexy eyes kept meeting mine. Quite incredible, for women didn't have to look at you, did they? They could look somewhere else, self-contained and bored. But we had things to talk about, simple things. Life at Berkeley was winding down for both of us. We were seniors, atop the plateau, looking over the wall. She was considering graduate school. I was considering, well, just considering. Something would come next. For now, there was this. And this was everything. A woman so adult and so charged with sensuality, quietly sitting with me in a coffee shop booth. And I wasn't so overpoweringly afraid of her that I had to shrink and run away. And she kept looking at me and we kept talking about the strangeness of student life ending. As though we understood each other and always had.

And a woman like this with her steady warmth and inner peace, choosing to spend her time with me, well it was inexplicable. Yet it was. And I didn't need the Geary Theater or even San Francisco to impress her, because I didn't need to impress her. I didn't need anything and did not have to do anything but sit here. And why had something so simple taken so long?

What were women like? I wanted to know this too...being so uncool, but the way she kept looking at me said ask away. So, these days, tell me, Judith, how is it for you, as a woman? I did not know what I was asking, but it sounded convincingly hip and sophisticated, this question. Well, Judith said as she clicked down her spoon on the saucer, one of the big differences is the pill. Women didn't have to worry about having sex as much as they used to. I nodded knowingly.

So far, things had gone okay, and maybe more than okay. She was still talking to me, smiling at me, looking at me. I hadn't bored her. Always a distinct possibility in the back of my mind. And now this chitchat about women and having sex... god, what a thrilling possibility. A possibility that seemed as real and inviting as a warm slice of pie, pastry all crumbling and ice cream melting. Everything was melting. Ideas about what I was and how I would be on a date. I had a car, the night was young, so why not head back to Berkeley? What next? What incredible, joyously ordinary thing next?

Driving up Shattuck Avenue, nearing my room, it occurred to me. Food. We really hadn't eaten. How about some pizza? The whole thing was so unlikely, the two of us walking up my stairs at almost midnight, me carrying the hot cardboard box. The two of us sitting on my carpet, my back against the bed, Judith's feet curled under her. Eating the hot, melting, greasy slices. A knot of fear slid up my chest as the pizza slid down. We were running out of pizza, running out of clear activity, and this other thing was looming. The thing that was so much easier now that there was the pill. Which, one never knew, might be just as easy and free of fear as the pill itself. All one needed was a glass of water and a gulp. I headed to the kitchen. When I came back, Judith had her shoes off. She drank some water. I had some too. We sat on the bed, side by side. I put my arm around her. Should I say something? No, do something. Hug her, no, kiss her. Where? Cheek first? No, she had already determined that, and there was nothing for me to do but fall backwards on the bed. Judith lay on top of me, her capacity for kissing astonishing. She had me pinned, it seemed, much like wrestling my brother. Overpowered, on my back, and Judith's excitement at kissing became downright frightening. I turned on my side, wondering how it was done, kissing and relaxing at the same time.

Judith was breathing heavily, thrusting her hips hard at me. Sharp bones, aggression driving out the warm physical enthusiasm. What to do? I knew what people did. They took off their clothes. Act like you know what you're doing. I sat up. Judith surprised me by helping remove my trousers. Because I didn't know how? Never mind. Act like it's normal. And dammit if we weren't naked. Naked and in bed, side-by-side again. Judith's breasts. This upward curve, the nipples. Were her breasts big or small? I was supposed to know, and not to stare like an idiot. Act like you know what you're doing. I had gotten this far, after all, and now it was a matter of will. Courage, determination, control. And not giving up. Judith didn't need to know about my embarrassing feelings, my overripe virginity. This was my chance, and it was up to me. Which meant lying here... and what... sucking the breasts.

Judith's hand on my head. Paul, you're hurting me. Oh, my God, how stupid. I stopped. Judith's hand was on my penis, softly dangling, even shrinking. The opposite of what normally happened. The opposite of getting hard and the man putting it in, putting it to her. Nowhere to hide, nowhere to go. What to say? Sorry, I said. Sorry. Judith turned and looked at me steadily, not flinching. These breasts that curved this way, with the force of a small ski jump, and the nipples and the pubic hair. And me, stupid, an idiot. Let's get some sleep, Judith said. A reprieve. Things would be better in the morning. Things were always better in the morning.

But they weren't. Judith and I got up. We dressed, and I found some food. And we walked outside. It was December, smoke curling from neighborhood chimneys, the brick and the shingled houses. The desert so far away. And we walked side by side, saying very little. I couldn't understand why she was there. Maybe she wanted to be. Another date. I asked for another date. Another chance. Because everything was fine, except for one thing. One surprisingly small and soft thing. I wasn't working at this enough or wasn't working in the right way. A fear was rising. Judith would realize the truth and find out who I really was. An incompetent, worse than an idiot. Someone who didn't have it.

She'd had it, in fact, had everything. And we'd had a date. Then we'd had another. Even a third date. Consistent effort, as life often demanded. And though my body wasn't working, Judith's was. Somehow, my fumblings managed to arouse her. Clutching my hand and holding my head, she whispered hot in my ear, "I want to say I love you."

I stopped. Everything pulled in, pulled away. For this could not be true. My heart clenched like a fist. A tear rolled down her cheek to mine. What on earth was wrong with me? Why couldn't I say something? This was the very thing life was about, this thing she had offered. This is what I had always believed. And now, I couldn't believe it. Judith was fooling me. The moment expanded, saddened. I was resigned, closed and steely. I stared at the ceiling. I said nothing.

But Judith did the next morning. She'd gotten up, dressed, brushed her hair. I enjoyed watching all these things, having never seen them before. But I was seeing something different now, a briskness, a purpose. Sorry, she couldn't stay this morning. She had things to do. It was my turn to use the bathroom, and I got up to put on my robe for the walk down the common hallway. Wait, she said, her tone flat and not inviting. I sat down.

You don't really like women, she said. You really don't. She smiled sadly, knowingly. Things were so different, so animate with a woman in my room, and I was getting almost used to it. For the moment, all I could take in was her. How she moved with both grace and a flat-footedness that made her human, accessible. That I had grown accustomed to Judith placing her hands behind her back, lowering her gaze and gently padding forward to say something. Her approach sent shivers of fear through me, yet her intent came through. She wanted to reach me, not to threaten. My antic façade had crumbled in the last few weeks, but I had had a woman in my room and even in my bed. I saw this all in an instant and understood that when the instant was over, something empty and leaden would take its place. That thing rose like death. It sucked the day out of the room. Panic clenched, and I could not speak. This was going to happen. It was happening as Judith muttered good-bye and the door shut.

In Spanish III

NOVEMBER 2005

It was winter quarter at Berkeley, days lengthening, sun low slanting, and all I wanted was out. Impotent. If the word did not take prominence in my mind, its meaning did. Judith knew. No one else needed to. Perhaps there was a way forward. I seemed to have found it. Keep to the edges and aim at June. Graduation would force a change. Something different would follow. For now, it was head down, in and out of classes, moving through campus at the safe fringe of the crowds. Bumping into Judith, looking up and seeing her unexpectedly, the hollowing shame of it... I would avoid this. Just a matter of staying alert, keeping to the edges.

Once, wandering out of Restoration Drama, I saw, or thought I saw, Judith's head moving with the throng. She appeared to be with others, her expression troubled. I looked away. She had not seen me, I was almost certain. How odd, my momentary glimpse of her. Troubled... over me? No, only in my self-flattering dreams. She was a strong, independent young woman in search of love. She had wasted time with me and had moved on. I had moved into the shadows, the winter shadows, which would disappear. I would disappear from Berkeley soon enough... and something, something less humiliating, would come next.

Spanish III was populated by juniors. I was secretly relieved to be with students who were slightly younger. The teacher had a light way in the classroom, sweeping us into conversation. In the past, the stumbling baby talk of language learning had embarrassed me. But here students joked, fumbled, forgave... and talked.

In Spanish III we even rehearsed a skit, our collective oral exam. It was an Andalusian melodrama, some gaslight play of the hiss-the-villain era. I was the jilted husband who confronted the unfaithful wife, swore he had been cuckolded, and whipped out a pistol. The woman pleaded for her virtue. The husband shot her, then realized his folly. Finito. I had been only so-so at Spanish, but I found my voice in this role. The lines came easily to memory, and my pronunciation improved with each run-through. The kids watching my performance laughed. I laughed with them. We were safely inside, in a classroom, far from anywhere that Judith might see.

Our skit needed something. I had seen the drama department's prop gun fire in a Brecht play. Why not ask? A drama teaching assistant sent me off with the thing, more or less a cap pistol. At the next rehearsal, I told the cast there was going to be a realistic touch. We proceeded as usual, all of us pacing about the front of the classroom pulling exaggerated poses, milking the stilted story for all it was worth. When my turn came to face the unfaithful wife, my costar, a Chinese-American girl named Karen, quivered out her line "una pistola?" I said something broadly ironic about "la muerte," and fired. Karen raised her hands to her face, stunned and at the edge of tears, a new dramatic height. The cast applauded. The director slapped me on the back.

The rehearsal over, I assembled my pile of books. Karen stood before me, mute, breathing heavily. Please don't use that gun, she said, her eyes all terror. Please. I stormed outside. It was an inspired touch, the gun. It was my touch, and I'd had my moment. And at this moment, I didn't care who saw me standing in front of Dwinelle Hall, even Judith. We all needed moments. And silly, quivering Karen wasn't going to ruin mine.

On the day of the production, the Spanish III sections crowded into one large classroom, people jammed among the desks. The teaching assistants had spread out cake, paper plates and napkins on a table near the back. Our teacher uttered the Spanish words for let the play begin, and so it did. The cast was better than ever, the audience laughter unexpected and its effect buoyant. I not only paced through my melodramatic moments, but strutted. The teaching assistants howled. The big climax approached, and fortunately the pistol was small and easily concealed in my pants pocket. Bang. The noise was louder than the laughter, and this time Karen responded with utterly convincing tears. Wild applause ensued, and I regretted not planning for a curtain call. The teacher handed me a piece of cake, the room buzzed, and I buzzed too. I could do something, be part of something, be spontaneous, even joyous. The classroom began to empty, and I headed for the drama department to return the gun.

Karen stepped out of a doorway. I barely recognized her, so swollen were her eyes. She rubbed away the tears and directed her quavering voice at me. You are an awful person, she said. I stared at her steely, hard and uncaring. I'd heard all this before. Abandoning my father, wounding my mother, the disloyal son who thought only of himself, the awful person. Now I kept on walking, a knot of guilt pulling at my chest, but something angry pulling me also. I wasn't going to stand for this. I wasn't even going to hear it. I certainly wasn't going to apologize. I'd been apologizing all my life.

It was June now every day, particularly Saturday. Only a week or so left, Redwood pollen slanting through the shafts of sunlight, the campus creek tinkling. I strolled beside the stream. A break from the library, one of those out-of-the-way campus paths, and the mind needed sunlight. I checked my watch. A twenty-minute break, then back to cramming. I caught a glimpse of something familiar, a languid, strolling gait... Judith. She was walking toward me, just a few feet away. She smiled. I had forgotten all this about her, the quiet warmth, the beauty. How are you? How are you? Fine. Fine. Well.... Well.... About to go our separate ways, of course. And it hit me. The free tickets to a rock concert someone had given me. I could go alone, of course. But wouldn't. Besides, it was finals week and... well, here were the tickets and here came the words. Did she want to go? And her "no" came gently, easily. I took in Judith's expression. Not unkind, only firm. As one might be with a child. Well. Well. I headed for the library.

A June Night

NOVEMBER 2005

I wasn't entirely cynical about it back then, even as a senior when it was fashionable to be sick of studies. In fact, I'd been studying pretty hard that June night in 1968. When the Berkeley student union shut, I quickly walked across the campus, sticking to the lighted paths. Steam rose ghostly from grates and a faint mechanical hum emanated from buildings where generators, pumps and mechanisms kept Coca-Cola bottles chilled and laboratories alive. Moving through the darkest places, I occupied myself with thoughts of the defeat of nature, how night revealed the University's urban underpinnings, with Strawberry Creek and its redwood banks reduced to Central Park. I had been studying for the last final of college.

Striding up Spruce Street into the North Berkeley Hills, passing storybook houses, I recited the last of the verb endings for my Spanish III final. Was it too late to stop at Jim and Patsy's? Maybe so. Jim and Patsy, like all around me, were drawing inward, becoming couples, preparing to move on.

"Hey, man." This from someone up ahead. I'd passed Virginia Street and was about to cross Cedar Street when three young men walked toward me. They were black, two with bandannas covering their heads, one nattily attired like a racetrack gent. "You got any money?" At this I smiled and shook my head. Everyone in Berkeley wanted spare change. Something collided with my chin. It took a moment to accept that it was a fist. Something salty filled my mouth, along with a loose piece of something sharp. The night, my brisk stroll, everything had stopped. The young men stood waiting. One of them grinned proudly. He was showing me something. It was shiny, silvery like a cap pistol. Guns, real guns like the ones I'd seen on television, were dark, dull metal. I was not going to be fooled and stepped toward the safety of the streetlight. With the bang, which was not terribly loud, my step ceased. Things descended with the gravitational precision of a stage curtain. My puppet body slipped downward, strings cut. The head bounced, then settled in a field of black rocks, the view of an eye resting on pavement.

The head, my head, lifted slightly. Now it was flung, the back of it scraping over the hard roughness below. As the head jerked forward an action shot rolled into view, a foot kicking at my belly. Now I understood that this body, my body, was presumed to be dead, and it was being moved into the shadows, out of sight. The jerking continued, my unfeeling body advancing over the pavement. I recognized a kick to the stomach, not from the impact, but from the aftermath of diaphragm gaspings. Now there was air, welcome air, and with it the panicky knowledge that I had not been breathing. I moaned something, "help." Footsteps disappeared into the night. A moment, then another "help."

I raised my head. I had heard the shot and knew approximately what had happened, but there was no explaining why nothing moved but my head. Shock. Perhaps people felt like this in massive shock. People who were dying. "Help." There was so little air. Compared to the distant sounds of traffic on Shattuck Avenue three blocks away, my moans were barely audible. Too little sound. Too late. "Help." Worth another try, or was it? Perhaps it was better to conserve energy. This had been a sad life, and this was a sad end. I raised my head again. I knew now that I was positioned under oleander bushes lining a neighborhood church. I could see the sidewalk. But it was very late. There were no cars.

No one walking. And I was very tired. Understandable that one could be sleepy after something like this. Rest was healing. And it had all been very sad… and it was night… and I had the right to sleep.

"Help." I was not going to stop. "Help." I was not. "Help." There were still possibilities. "Help." Even without enough air, or enough volume, this would have to do… futile, incessant…. "Help." A door banged open across the street. Footsteps. Feet scraping by me. The rough softness of a blanket on my neck. Someone crouched down slowly, the way old people did. "It's okay," he said, "an ambulance is coming." Which I could hear, because I was right on the ground where sirens skimmed over the earth, and could see when red swept, lighthouse-style, over the pavement.

Inside the ambulance, the world was surprisingly bright. I told the white-clad attendant I was afraid of dying. "It's a good sign that you're talking," he said.

On a gurney in the student hospital, a police detective leaned over me. He understood, he said, so many drug deals went awry. Who was it, he asked? I told him I had been studying my Spanish. He asked me again, and now I understood that this was my body, my energy, my life. It would be spent or conserved. I would talk to this detective later, or I would not. When a photographer leaned directly over my face with a massive camera and exploded a series of flash bulbs inches from my eye, I decided this was the ultimate indignity and let myself sleep.

When I awoke it was morning and my divorced parents, unaccountably together, stood at the foot of my bed. Everyone was smiling, except for the neurosurgeon who told me about the bullet in the spinal cord. Yes, he said, I was paralyzed from the neck down right now, but perhaps not forever. I did not know what to say. And it was hard to speak with spinal fluid running out my nose. A nurse asked if I wanted my hands on top of the sheet or under the sheet. I thought she was mad. Until I tried to move my arms.

In the Garden

Agriculture

APRIL 2005

These days, the big news is little. And entirely agricultural. Not to mention boxed in. I am acquiring a garden. Actually, I've been down this horticultural road before. I had a garden during the era of the first marriage. I recalled spending many lonely hours surrounded by raised beds. Interspersed with lonely hours in the marital bed. You make your bed, you lie in it, and you watch your garden grow.

I am not entirely certain what the current garden has grown from. I am no longer a landowner. It is my landlord who has sanctioned the construction of two redwood planter boxes at the end of his fourplex. Right at the end of the building, at the convergence of a mid-1950s apartment house, a late 1940s retirement home over the back fence and the sagging limbs of a massive oak tree. Actually, the latter are rapidly disappearing. My friend Robert has been assaulting them with an escalating arsenal of chainsaw weaponry. He's building these boxes. He's determined. He understands the mission. Get the crippled guy into agricultural production. He understands the reason. Salvation. Voltaire had it right. Fight the battles, betray and be betrayed, then retire to hoe your plot of earth. If it was good enough for Candide, it's good enough for me.

Robert's raised beds do reflect the changing times. They are twice as high as the ones I tended a decade ago. I simply cannot bend over as far as I used to. And they are designed for wheelchair access. There's not going to be a lot of walking around these beds. This is going to be a predominantly sedentary form of agriculture. Though I can gauge my neuromuscular losses in the new design of the raised earth beds, the prospect of gardening activity has already captured my spirit. Even without sighting a single one, I've already entered into combat with snails. It's survival, the law of the jungle, survival of the agricultural fittest. And I'm not yielding any precious ground to these mollusks. Before a single shovelful of soil has even gone into the planters, I've got the snail defenses in place. Long strips of copper, biochemical snail hell. Cross this line, you slimy fuckers. Make my day.

In my mind, I can already see the amber waves of grain, the bursting leaves of green, the rows and sheaves of my crops. Lettuce can hardly fail to impress. Particularly varieties like Rouge d'Hiver, which has the approximate consistency of crêpe paper and falls upon the plate like a languid ballet dancer. Surprising the quantity of plum tomatoes one can generate for cooking and drying. Not to mention basil. Carrots. And when it's time to bring out the big guns, corn. Until, rolling into the autumn, production begins to wane, the cover crop takes over and then in the dead of winter, garlic and seed potatoes go underground. Growing against all odds. Until it's spring again.

All the more appreciated, and a little poignant and bittersweet, from a wheelchair. And it is this sensibility that makes me forget the crop and the winter and even the snails to participate in the now, and the Robert, and the building of the beds. Because I have a tendency to hurry through my days, endlessly disappointed at my own limits and how long it takes me to do things for work, so that I not only miss the raising of the garden, but I fail to participate. For Robert knows what he's doing. He has had his own losses, his own midlife setbacks, and he understands why a crippled man needs to watch a garden grow. Just as I understand that Robert needs to build this garden at his current pace. He's in between things. And the garden work goes on in between those in-between things. I keep looking at the lengthening days, and my agricultural impatience mounts. But I understand. Robert is putting love into this work. Which is something you can't really buy. And certainly can't hurry.

Which is why on this day, near the end of the building, on the eve of having a big dump truck bring the soil in from Redwood City, it's important to participate. Which means Robert and I will drive to Home Depot. Or I'll just hang out with him as he saws and joins. With a disability, it is very easy to get habituated to being an observer. You don't, and you can't, do much of your own work. There's no changing oil or hanging sheet rock. Able-bodied people do these things. They do them for you. Which isolates you from the essential activities of life. And cuts you off from life's essentially active people. The workers. The doers. Those who build, and tend, and renew our material world. Particularly those who choose to hammer and rake and haul by choice. Like Robert, who's got a Ph.D. and years of professional research in his not-too-distant past. And now chooses to watch his carpentry grow, just as I plan to observe my garden. Men have camaraderie around building and fixing. It's something I've missed. So it's a perfect time, late middle age, to rediscover male construction space. A rediscovery, like everything in a disabled life, comes too little, too late. And like young lettuce leaves, carrot sprouts and, yes, weeds... right on time.

Sunflowers

MAY 2005

There's a definite coffin-like, sarcophagus quality to them. And at the same time they are what they are, botanical blank slates, empty, raised garden beds. Ready for planting. Ready for me. I wasn't quite ready for them.

Dutifully, I headed for the Palo Alto organic garden shop I frequented years ago. It has moved across the street, its hippie roots absent in the spacious brick quarters and the surprisingly high prices. $4.25 for a single sunflower seedling in a plastic pot? Absolutely. They are nonprofit, Common Ground. I am a nonprofit too. That's our common ground. Besides, what the hell, maybe it really does matter if you give money to people with aspirations to reduce the chemical impact, human footprint and general swath cut by homo sapiens as we wander about the land.

So there they were, new nursery plants, in the back of my wheelchair van, headed for my wheelchair-ramp-equipped apartment, which is now adjacent to two large wheelchair-height planter boxes. My wife set the plants on the boxes, then went about helping me. I bristled. This was going to be my domain. I surveyed my planter-box kingdom, determining the general plan. Height. One had to remember the height of various plants. I hadn't thought about this sort of thing in twelve years. The last time I'd had a disabled garden, I hadn't been in a wheelchair, and the raised beds were half the height of these. I'd spend many lonely hours sitting in folding chairs and crutching about, as I tended to the tomatoes and corn and lettuce. The more the plants thrived, the more my marriage withered.

Which, of course was then, and this was now. Marlou got the message quickly enough...let her second husband fumble about in his quadriparetic way with the sunflowers. And, surprise, my second wife seemed to understand. This wasn't about efficiency. One-handed, wheelchair-mechanized agriculture is a low-productivity endeavor. So, okay, in the twelve years since I had last hoed and raked and shoveled, muscles and nerves and joints had realigned. I couldn't really reach the far side of one gardening bed and, no, I didn't want Marlou reaching for me. But I did possess a hoe, which, without a word, she placed next to my wheelchair. This annoyed me, in the way a surgeon might be offended if he didn't get a chance to say "scalpel," like in the movies, and the damn thing just appeared on his instrument tray.

Well, the hoe wasn't quite the right instrument for digging, but, like so many things in a disabled life, it would do. I carved out enough earth to insert the first sunflower plant, then, with the hole almost out of reach, had to more or less hurl the plant into place. I maneuvered it upright with the hoe and then tamped the earth into place. One down, four to go. I had bought five seedlings, because...well, because of nothing. I'd come from work, a half-day meeting, and stopped in at the garden shop, tired and impatient. A warm spring day, the first, really, all year, and local gardeners had ravaged the plant stock. There were just odds and ends left. Two sunflowers of one type, and two of another variety, and one of another. It was all terribly inconsistent, unplanned and, yet, at home and facing the expanse of empty planter, I saw a solution. Plant the odd lone plant in the middle, then put two of one variety next to it, two of the others next to them. Thus, gardening. Improvisation. Symmetry redefined. Symmetry abandoned.

Still, despite the joy in this long-awaited moment, the incredible apartment birth of a wheelchair garden, A Tree Grows in Brooklyn, A Garden Grows in Menlo, I kept thinking of the past. The wife who was either absent or wouldn't listen...or the husband who was passive and wouldn't speak up. And, of course, the body that had declined so much. Which was why I decided that planting five sunflowers was enough. Yes, there was a big flat full of lettuce plants and basil, tomatoes and squash waiting to go into the ground. But I was waiting to go inside. I'd had enough. And I still had to exercise, to have Marlou strap my leg onto a stationary bicycle and pedal my way to cardiovascular health.

While she strapped, I talked. I told her it was a bittersweet experience, this reencounter with gardening, tinged with loss and regret. And she began to talk, for the first time in days, about frustrations in her life. So we had this. A marriage. My body was failing, and time was passing, and it wasn't entirely clear how long it would take to plant the rest of the vegetables. But late in life, I was acquiring sense. Or maybe I was acquiring life. I began my half-hour on the Exercycle, thinking of next steps. The eggplant. I promised my landlord I would grow one for him. And for Marlou, who likes eggplant too. For I felt like I'd walked into a clearing in a dark forest, after a long and futile journey, only to discover there was an open, sunlit place. And that a relationship, and life itself, aren't just an ordeal. And through the strangest of circumstances, a landless, single quadriplegic in an apartment can end up coupled, rooted and growing.

Raising Beds

AUGUST 2005

It was sometime in the spring, gazing out my apartment window, that my old man's fancy turned to thoughts of raised beds. In the olden days, when I was married the first time and living in an in-laws-financed starter home that proved to be a finisher home, I had a garden. It was behind the garage in that, my first, and only, house. In three raised beds, I cranked out an abundance of tomatoes, lettuce, corn and odd yuppie salad greens. I spent hours out there alone, sitting on a low stool, sometimes standing. All that garden solitude had much to do with the poor state of my marriage and the robustness of my body. So this spring, having by now abandoned further thoughts of house ownership in the Bay Area, and finding marriage and body conditions symmetrically reversed, I had a chat with my landlord. He surrendered a portion of lawn that had died in one of California's droughts, and so, with help from a carpenter friend, I was back in agricultural business.

Of course, because I'm in a wheelchair these days, the beds are more than raised. They are elevated, twice as high as their predecessors, and working on them involves more wheelchair maneuvering, less bending and standing. There's still plenty that's enlivening about growing your own lettuce. I calm myself by watering the seedlings, removing the weeds, tying the tomato vines to their poles. But the almost compulsive energy that made me build these raised beds in the first place has oddly vanished.

True, I've got plans. Cover crop in the autumn. Potatoes in January. Spinach by March. And then there are the gophers. They appeared one day quite unexpectedly, in the manner of all plagues. Having little sense of zoning or property rights, they had the wisdom to burrow from the adjoining lot's empty space behind a senior center, under the fence and into my corn patch. I saw the furrows and door mounds that signal their construction and felt a momentary sense of defeat. But then I sprang into quadriplegic action. That is to say, my wife and I did. And my carpenter friend. With a garden hose, we washed open the holes, dumped poison underground, sealed up the holes and went about our lives. I purchased two battery-powered ultrasonic guaranteed-to-drive-away-gophers beeping devices. I was not obsessing.

Of course, it's hard to say if the gophers have actually been driven away or found greener pastures. The latter may now be over the back fence, where the senior center has recently installed raised beds not unlike my own. For some time, one of the center's personal volunteers has wandered by my garden on a daily basis. I've urged him to get the center to build beds like my own, to make gardening more accessible to the senior masses. He assured me that he would pass on the word. And it appears that he did. An aerial view would reveal a procession of raised beds nominally separated by a fence. I'm not quite sure how the idea spread from one property to the next. Or even if it's an idea. Raising things to eat from the earth must be in our bones. It's more like a primal headline. RAISED BEDS – QUICKLY SPREADS. In a way, there's more pleasure from the spread of the beds than the actual beds.

Inverness Redux

APRIL 2007

The couple strolling down the shared dock of our Inverness cottage walk, dress and talk like tourists. From our wooden deck I watch them ascend the three ramshackle steps from their wooden deck. Seeing me, the middle-aged man, shirt and trousers bulging in a way that is becoming all too familiar, asks if I mind. No, I tell them, it's yours, it's ours. Two rented cottages, side by side, sharing a single splintering boardwalk. Okay, they say, trundling off. I shake my head in disbelief. How did Inverness get this way? And what is "this way"? Furthermore, what better "way" should Inverness get?

First, go to the original. Inverness, Invernesshire, about 1980 via British Rail. By the time you arrive, at least you'll know why so many Britons were not sorry, initially, to see the last of their state railways. For our visit, the overnight sleeper left Euston Station around 10 p.m. At dawn it entered the Scottish Highlands, where a lone buck stood proud beside the hilly tracks showing off its antlers as if posing for a whiskey label. There was no dining car on the train, so it was a good thing we were due at Inverness early. And equally unfortunate when the train came to a permanent halt. An hour went by, a long time on a British train... though admittedly nothing on, say, Amtrak. I got dressed and hobbled down the corridor in search of someone who knew something. A young man wearing a badly stained British Rail jacket brushed by me in the corridor. He was not about to make eye contact but was not above body contact, being grossly overweight. And being in a British-Rail-savvy frame of mind, I more or less shouted my question into his face: Why were we stopped? He emitted three syllables. Loco's bust.

Did this sour me on Inverness, Scotland? By the time I got there, I was starving. With the train from London arriving late, the northbound departure for Wick was delayed. Not by much, mind you, but barely enough time for a starving cripple to wander out to the street and get a brief look at the center of Inverness. Yes, the skies were gray. This was Scotland, after all. But so was the mood. The low stone buildings seemed to have escaped decades of British anti-soot scrubbings. People scurried about the streets looking poor and rather downtrodden. The shops had modest goods; the restaurants were dire. I did what any sensible traveler would do. I bought a Cadbury's whole nut bar and headed back to the train station. Inverness, 1980.

Inverness, California, 2007. It's impossible to say what the two Invernesses share except, maybe, Scotch Broom. The latter is abloom in naughty yellow up and down the California coast, though because it's an invasive species, we shun it. We disapprove of it. We denounce it. Aside from this roadside shrub, the two towns may have shared, at one point, a certain genteel poverty. This is only a guess, but I know there was a time when Inverness had nothing fancy. As a university student, I found the town to be a place to buy a sandwich on the way to the newly opened Point Reyes National Seashore. The latter was something of an experiment in the National Park system, mixing wild and agricultural lands in one preserve. With the winding roads, getting there wasn't as easy as other Bay Area beaches. The Seashore attracted few visitors at first, and some thought it was a joke. In August 1967, the *San Francisco Chronicle* ran a front-page photo of South Beach, one of the parking-lot-and-picnic-spot developments awaiting the tourist crowds. The South Beach parking lot was completely empty.

Nowadays Point Reyes is thick with hikers, campsites full all summer, so many tourists clamoring to see the lighthouse that the park has created a special shuttle. You leave your car at, yes, South Beach, if there's a space. You'd think that Inverness could easily swell to meet the tourist challenge. But swelling is not what Inverness is all about. Quelling is the Inverness thing. The restrictions on development along Tomales Bay are so tight that nothing has gone up near the water in years. The water, shallow, oyster-laden and very tidal, still laps against remarkably empty shores.

It must be the roll of the green hills and the inland reach of the bay in its elongated rift valley that convinced someone that this was like Scotland. A loch in the Highlands. A fanciful notion that just doesn't work with California poppies roadside, the smell of laurel, the red curling bark of madrone and tiny eateries displaying historic photos of before and after the last big earthquake on the San Andreas Fault, beneath the bay.

But the genteel poverty thing, that seems worth exploring. When I first saw Inverness in the late 1960s the place was known as a weekend getaway for Berkeley professors. Many owned cabins there, modest wooden-slatted cabins that might, or might not, have a refrigerator. With its shade and fog and cool summers, Inverness was no place to get a tan. It was a place to get away. From students, from traffic, from one's routine. To... a place that was cool, vaguely ramshackle, anything but haute. To... now. A place where true strangers rent cabins side by side and barely say hello. I don't believe that was the Inverness of the old days. And in this sense, Inverness has grown poorer as it has grown richer.

And how did the place get richer? Oh, exploding Bay Area property values, I suppose. The eventual popularity of Point Reyes. And preservation itself. The shack, a.k.a. cottage, we recently rented on the web from the unseen proprietor of a bed and breakfast in Point Reyes ran to two hundred dollars a night. Unfortunately, I believe this attracts people who like being around two-hundred-dollars-a-night people. This may explain why our neighbors didn't speak to us. They have the idea – or is it my idea? – that Inverness is exclusive. Which it is. The town's having excluded development along the fragile bay, and the fragile hills fronting the fragile bay, not to mention the fragile farmlands beyond the hills and the fragile watershed beyond all that, makes Walt's shack exclusive in a supply-and-demand sort of way. Too bad the track lights in the bedroom don't work, and the two reading lamps in the front room might be good for casting a fishing line, but not a light... both lamps being either burned out or inoperative.

Though actually I am of two minds about the lights and the bad mattress and the bathroom off the kitchen, not to mention the dusty soup cans at the Inverness Store a few yards down the highway, not to mention the appalling goulash ladled up across the street at Vladimir's Czech restaurant, now $26 prix fixe, paper napkins included. I hope people get tired of Inverness, at least the wrong kind of people. I want the right kind of people there. I want us there. Marlou and me. It's our kind of place.

Which makes me grateful for my modest yet sustained income rolling in from a disability insurance company somewhere in the Midwest. And the health plan without which the insurance checks would be a risible drop in life's bucket. And the fact that I am alive to enjoy all this. And so is Marlou.

In early afternoon, when my van pulled into its parking space by our apartment, fresh from Inverness, my shoulder and neck not hurting too much from the two-hour drive, we entered our home just long enough to down some takeout sushi and say goodbye. Marlou had her appointment with the surgeon, the one who's going to remove a rather large chunk of her liver. It's a renewable resource, liver. And so is the spirit. And so is Inverness, which keeps renewing itself and renewing us.

Someday the renewing will stop. But not in my day. No matter how many days I have left, the West Marin Agricultural Land Trust can be, well, trusted. To its trustees. Just as our cottage neighbors can be trusted to wander down our Tomales Bay dock all snooty and aloof. Classy soap they've got in their bathroom, transparent and glycerin and wrapped in a custom bed-and-breakfast label. It's okay. Cancer hasn't stopped us, and the cottage neighbors won't either. We, and Inverness itself, will deal with them later.

Inverness

AUGUST 2006

The news crept in with the morning light. Outside, the fog hung sad over the tan oaks and scrubby laurel. What was one to do? Marlou stood in the doorway quietly explaining what had happened. I sought some deeper answer in her eyes. But there was nothing, only the resigned air of someone who has witnessed loss before. She said it again. There would be no foam. This was to be, from its start to its conclusion, a bad foam day. Something passed between us, the knowledge that as the espresso machine had hissed like the pneumatic brakes of a slowing train and both of us had seen that milky froth even before we fully saw each other, caffeine still being absent in our systems, the promise was not to be fulfilled. Something had failed. And so, something failed and faltered within me. No foam. There would be no milky foam. On some days, the Italian coffee machine failed to deliver. This was one of those. Nothing more needed to be said. Nothing more than everything. I wanted to tell Marlou about the dampening of desire, the muting of possibilities, of hopes thwarted, of promises shipped to the wrong address. No foam. No effervescence. None of that quality attributed to the bubbly personality. There would be no bubbles. No foam.

The range of disappointments possible in Inverness, California, is rather slim. Failure to foam is about as bad as it gets. It gets foggy, then it gets sunny, then it gets foggy. But it never gets old. Only I do that. And Inverness is where I do it best. If I had the money, I would do it here forever. Why Inverness? I don't know. It's beyond knowing. Actually, no one does know about it. Inverness has escaped the notice of virtually everyone, even in the Bay Area. Only hardened introverts know it. Unfortunately, there are just enough of these to drive up the price of vacation real estate to ludicrous levels. We have rented a house for two weeks. Small decks hang off either end of the place like flaps on an inexplicably double envelope. And the whole thing sits up on poles, being a pole house. The usual hillside trees pose at the windows, limbs held high and formal, framing everything. Particularly the bay. Did I mention Tomales Bay? It's out there shimmering and beckoning all day long.

Why Inverness? God only knows where the name came from. But suffice it to say, once the Scots got out of the Highlands, there was no stopping them. So why not head for Point Reyes, abandoned, windswept and devoted from its earliest settlement to the raising of cows? A situation that, in spirit, matches the Scottish experience. And never mind if the details are little off. No, it doesn't look like Scotland. The real Inverness is much grayer and bleaker. Certainly, Tomales Bay doesn't remotely resemble a loch. In fact, the bay is quintessentially Californian. Treeless hills on one side, green or brown depending on the season, forest on the other. Actually, it's a thin, even scrubby forest. Bishop Pines, a rare and rather primitive looking breed, work their way down the hillside. The hillside is straight as a line, and so is the bay. Both share precisely the same geological origin. The San Andreas Fault runs under the water, making a beeline for the

Pacific Ocean, where it disappears from sight. But not from mind. Evidence of earthquakes is all around Inverness. The temblors are fêted at the national park visitor center, the tiny Inverness museum, and on the walls of any local restaurant worth its salt.

Our rented house, sitting up on its foundation poles, holds itself proudly, as though to say "this is enough." So forget the television. There isn't one. And you can largely forget the Internet, as well, unless you want to watch your life move before you at dial-up speed. So, you get up, deal with the loss of foam and get on with the day. The day being rather like the night, except brighter. You will be brighter too if you have been reading. If not, you will be duller. Which will force you to contemplate the bay, spending hours counting sailboats. Followed by a long meditation upon the opposite shore where, maybe in those indistinct white shacks, locals sell oysters. Okay, so they're not really locals. They are probably advance agents from some huge Japanese cartel, quietly cornering the market on the Tomales Bay shellfish brand. But they seem like locals. And that's all that matters.

Inverness tends to be something of a disaster for disabled people. The houses are generally old, built on slopes, and the particulars of their accessibility or inaccessibility can never be determined through any means of remote communication. Never mind the pictures on the website. Forget a phone conversation with the realtor. The latter will only yield a chirpy description of "a short walk down a path." Which sums up our current circumstance. Though one should mention that the short walk is preceded by a harrowing drive up and down a one-way road, which eventually widens enough for cars to park on a bend. Followed by the descent of a virtual cliff. A walkway, more exactly a trail, traverses the slope from the road to the steps leading to the front door. On the day we arrived, two workmen patching up something at a neighboring house watched me attempt to maneuver the path in my electric wheelchair. Wielding a huge shovel of the sort that elsewhere clears snow, they gathered up huge shovelfuls of Inverness leaves, gradually revealing the powdery earth, one result of the eons of ground leaf dust, underneath. They cleared the way just enough for me, with their considerable help, to make it back up the trail and park the wheelchair permanently beside my van. Marlou threw a tarp over the wheelchair. That will keep raccoons, blue jays, neighborhood cats, foxes and squirrels off it. I will be using it only occasionally, mostly to load myself back into the van and drive somewhere. Not that I won't think twice about doing even that, descending the quadriplegic nightmare hill, my life and my Ford van hanging by the neurologically weakened powers of my left foot. On the brake.

Indoors, it's not a place for access. More steps from the front door, a full stairway down to the beds. Never mind. I come to Inverness to see everything change. To spend day after day hearing the breeze rustle through the trees, to answer approximately one phone call per week, to read, to think, to write. Supposedly to "slow down," although everything in my spirit speeds up. That is to say, things brighten, despite the losses of the day, such as the foam. That's as bad as it gets around here, no foam on the morning coffee. That and the weather, for some days the fog comes in too early and stays too late. Too late for what? I don't know. I'll spend the next ten days figuring that one out.

In Gretna, Louisiana
OCTOBER 2005

Note that if you ever get shot in the spine during a street robbery, there are people who will pay to fly your half-paralyzed self in the guise of a crime expert to New Orleans. Okay, so you'll have to wait thirty-five years. So what? You'll get to cross the Mississippi River on the Gretna Bridge, which locals call the Crescent City Bridge and the Federal Highway Department calls I-90, but any sensible person would call spectacular.

So what if two years later, on this bridge to the perfectly ordinary suburb of Gretna, police would be shooting over the heads of people fleeing the sewage swamp that had become New Orleans? Never mind that. Because in October 2003, there was only the present, with me and the driver of the airport van. He was a seventy-ish black man, aloof and formal, who couldn't see the flood coming, but knew what it would bring.

I'd never been in the South. I'd never seen the Mississippi. And there it was hundreds of feet below, a night river where sinister half-lit freighters loaded diamonds and nuclear gear headed for some secret Goldfinger island near the Bahamas.

Hard to say what brings a crippled crime victim to spend three days working with young criminal men. Including black teenagers like those who had shot me in the neck as I walked home from a university library. Those young criminals had never been caught. Which didn't mean they were free or even alive. Somewhere in Gretna a man I'd met at a conference ran a recovery program for prisoners emerging from Louisiana's notorious Angola State Penitentiary. We agreed, he and I, that it would be good for violent men to see the paralytic fruit of their labors.

All of which explains why, in early autumn in the Deep South, I was turning on the air conditioner in my motel room and watching a white swirl of condensation shoot from the vents. I looked out the window at Denny's across the parking lot. It was a restaurant. There was no other.

Forced to leave my two-hundred-pound electric wheelchair in California, I'd brought a manual version, handy for being pushed by airport attendants, but awkward and difficult to steer with one working arm. Heading for Denny's, I reverted to a technique from my hospital days, shoving myself backwards with my working leg. I wove between parked cars, occasionally turning to see where I was going. I shoved myself backwards up the curb ramp to the sidewalk, to Denny's.

The waitress who opened the door was black. All the waitresses were black, and all the patrons were white. The plastic menu contained nothing that wasn't fried. I ordered the fried fish. I wondered why I had come to this distant place to spend a solitary evening in a motel coffee shop where everything was sad. The Formica table. The large, doubtless poorly paid waitress shuttling between tables, too young to be so obese. I paid my bill. I slid from the Naugahyde booth and sat in my folding wheelchair.

Outside, it was remarkably dark for 8 p.m. I looked up at the stars and saw a boiling blackness of cloud. The curb ramp was steep. I took it slowly, wedging my foot against the asphalt, inching down the incline. A large warm plop hit my neck. I sighed and recalled my London youth, walking somewhere with a friend's father, an elegant Polish Jew. He stopped to brush bird poop from his hat, observing, "For the goyim, they sing."

Another warm plop, then another. A flock of birds. I touched my neck. Water. Inexplicably warm. And not falling in droplets, but more like water balloons, way beyond rain. Hundreds of California garden hoses in the sky disgorging tepid contents on the parking lot. Only a few yards from the restaurant now, I pushed hard with my working leg and pulled with my functioning arm. I was sodden within seconds. A wish to stay dry gave way to thoughts of not warping my leather belt. Water was rolling from my pants legs as from a rain gutter. I was a living rinse cycle. I was worrying about my shoes.

In the drowning distance, someone fled the restaurant, bursting through the door, running through the deluge. The waitress materialized. She ran like someone not accustomed to the practice. Someone who had missed out on most of Physical Education and all of girls' soccer. "Here," she said, seizing the handles of my wheelchair. I raised my leg and placed it on the foot pedal while she rolled me fast across the parking lot. She found the curb ramp and now we were up and out of the deluge. Water poured in sheets off the roof of the covered walkway.

I told her she had saved me. "That's all right," she said, "can you get in the room?" No problem, I told her. She looked skeptical. "You got your key?" I stood up and tried to wedge my hand through the pieces of wet fabric that had become my pocket. I gave her the key, and she opened the door. I had the thought, however fleeting, that she was planning to rob me. She pushed my wheelchair inside, dashed into the rain, and I sat in the open doorway watching her flail across the asphalt. All she needed was a little coaching to acquire a stride, lift the knees, coordinate the arms. But I knew she hadn't had coaching and a lot of other things.

People who have very little often give very much. And it is these people who define humanity. Who carry hope forward like Olympic runners with their torch. And because their flame is feeble and the distance far, they need encouragement. Not suspicious stares from a white guy who thinks he's maybe being robbed.

I did not sleep well that night. The next day, after spending hours in a circle with 40 recently released black convicts, I was glad to return my motel room. I tried to nap. At 6 p.m., I stood and wedged the door open with my crutch, struggling to shove the folded wheelchair outside. This disabled-accessible room was designed to drive handicapped persons insane. The high, mounded doorsill blocked the passage of any wheelchair, and the door spring felt more powerful than Moby Dick's flipper. But now I was outside, too tired to care, and it would be clear sailing to Denny's.

A man exiting the room next door offered to give me a push. Denny's? Wouldn't I rather join him at the shopping center across the street? Within minutes, I was ordering a gumbo and staring across a tablecloth at this guy who worked on an oil rig. While I ate the gumbo, he talked about where the oil was and where it wasn't and how tankers had changed. This was why God had invented extroverts, to give the rest of us a chance to eat and think. Spending the day with people who were black and poor, I'd found that all of us had lives. The men's Louisiana accents were almost incomprehensible. I felt the exhaustion of learning a foreign language.

One of the men was walking into the restaurant now, a handsome young black kid, not yet twenty. He spoke to the maître d'. My oil-rig companion leaned across the table. "That boy just came to the wrong restaurant." I was already waving at the kid. We'd just spent an uncomfortable day together and had a sort of bond. The young man smiled at me briefly, took his job application and departed. I thought of how it was to emerge from Angola Penitentiary and find one's way back to simple things, like washing dishes. Different from leaving a hospital crippled, but maybe not so different.

"You know him?" I told my dining companion yes, I'd been in a daylong workshop with black prisoners. He nodded, and recommended the bread pudding.

Bluetooth

FEBRUARY 2009

Einstein's universe may be forever expanding, but mine is both collapsing and enlarging at the same time. The simultaneity should trouble no one, for it is perfectly in sync with the relativistic theory of middle age, which has nothing to do with the middle, but defines itself as any point short of the end... of existence. Testing, one-two-three. This is the sound of a sixty-two-year-old mastering his Bluetooth headset. Thing is, anyone properly schooled in Grimm will want to know who Bluetooth is, his relationship to Bluebeard, and so on. They would be barking up the wrong technological tree, of course, but never mind. No one knows why the tooth is blue or why the chicken crossed the road. The point is he is there, at last in my ear, after many months on my desk.

Thing is, the last time the voice-recognition people phoned to make me an offer I couldn't refuse, I didn't refuse. I bought the latest version of their software, one Bluetooth headset and a Philips handheld digital recorder. The software is nothing new. I once ran a business on it. I write this blog on it. It is me, and I am it. People unfamiliar with my way of non-finger typing do not understand why voice-recognition breeds a whole new breed of error. Instead of typos – there's no typing – there are "voice-o's." If you are waxing Edwardian, for example, and say that someone engaged in "fisticuffs," the voice system likely will recognize "fizzie fucks." That's how it is. Warn your editor.

Voice-recognition requires a microphone, something worn on the head and plugged into the computer's USB port. This derives from an old military term, Un-Soldierly Behavior in Port, but never mind. The point is that the USB requires a wire, and you want to go wireless. You are sixty-two years old and you want to be a real cool no-wires kind of guy. You want to be like all the cool guys who stride out of high-rise buildings with inexplicable scarab beetle things stuck in their ears. You want one of these, because you think it will make you look like a bond trader. It will. Except that there aren't any bond traders anymore, but you can't master this fact until you master your headset.

Thing is, when the software package arrives, the promised Bluetooth arrives also, and without instructions. The latter are deemed unnecessary, because all the cool bond traders rip their Bluetooth headsets out of the bubble wrap, stick them in their ears and go to it. Just like my nephew knew how to work my plasma TV before I bought it. It's a young person's thing. If you're cool enough to be a bond trader, you work the trapeze without a net.

All of which explains why the Bluetooth microphone sat in its bubble wrap on my desk for six months before I summoned help. Naturally, the middle-aged friend who came by could not make the thing work either. He resorted to the web. And gradually all was revealed. The little flange on the side of the Bluetooth controls everything. Off/on, connection, volume. Press a certain way, and it works. Press wrong, and you might as well lie down in the middle of the street. But over time, trial by error teaches you the way of the Bluetooth button.

And now, this thing stuck prominently in my ear, I can roll over to Peet's and act cool. I can pretend that my discussions with the barista are actually turning up on a computer screen back home. The whole experience is cool beyond description. As for the Philips USB digital recorder, which purports to actually capture random thoughts at Peet's or anywhere, I plan to open the box and inspect this gadget sometime soon. Give it a few months.

This technology leap occurred at the same time as my sister's visit. She and her husband proved to be a marvelous catalyst in getting the two of us out. Under siege by cancer, Marlou tends to pull up the drawbridge and wait things out behind the battlements. We haven't been to a movie or gone for a purely nonmedical pleasure drive in quite a while. So, the four of us made it out, Susie and her husband, Andy, Marlou and me. To the Stanford Theatre. Over the hills to the coastal town of Pescadero. And then home, and out to the garden.

Of course, first came the garden center. I waited in the car while my sister purchased spinach, lettuce and flower seedlings. Back home, we prepared the beds. My raised beds inspire raised eyebrows in Marlou this time of year. The remnants of the cover crop and, worse, the non-composted remains of last year's broccoli and tomato vines stick out of the earth. Marlou always wants to tidy this stuff up, and we have an annual tug-of-war. But having given ground on all matters pertaining to carpet, I probably give off a certain vibe in the garden. Besides, my sister proved masterly at the wielding of two bags of Nurseryman's Magic Nutrient Mix. She placed each on the bed, ripped the plastic open lengthwise, like a surgeon doing a simultaneous appendectomy and heart bypass, and proceeded to spread the contents. Within minutes, there was barely a trace of cover crop, living or dead. The seedlings went into the ground. And we went inside. But not before one final act.

I'm not sure what possessed me to buy an industrial quantity of California poppy seeds. But I found the stuff on the Internet, and the minimal order was enough to cover half a block. So what? My sister loaded an old spice bottle with a shaker top and sprinkled the seeds around the unplanted bed. She put the unused poppy seeds back in the cardboard box with last year's remnants. And poked around the box. Which turned up a packet of mixed poppies. Not to mention lupine. And some foxglove. The seeds dated from the first Clinton administration. And, no, there were no jokes or even thoughts about anyone spreading their seed. It's just that the decade and a half had passed, and I was still here, and so were the seed packets. My sister opened them all, flung the contents over the bed, and then we went inside. To wait for dinner. Wait for the rain. To see what would come up.

Seeds

FEBRUARY 2007

I'm not sure what Avery was doing last summer when we jointly sowed our second crop of butter lettuce. We worked side by side, our sides being more or less at the same altitude when he stands and I sit in my wheelchair. As a nonparent, it seems surprisingly natural to get into joint activity mode with a child. Part teaching, part wildlife observation, with the exasperation potential always high...yet something flows like a river, something that tells you to forget the utility of the endeavor and tune in. If you want agricultural productivity, call Cargill. If you want agriculture at its least mechanized and most primal, call four-year-old Avery.

The problem with seeding a garden with your local preschooler is that in the end you have something pretty far from the original plan. So you have to let go of plans the way Avery lets go of seeds...totally and at the last moment. In fact, our lettuce seed was getting flung around so erratically that there came a point when I was more than happy to have Buffie, Avery's mother, take over. She shook out carrot seeds in neat rows, while talking to Avery, occasionally letting him hold part of the packet, but keeping her eye on the mission. Dammit if everything wasn't getting nurtured, botanical and human. No wonder the experience was inexplicably intense and exhausting. Still, something competitive in me was already relishing the day when I could pointedly eye the sprouting lettuce and muse aloud about the odd absence of carrots. The message being "Avery, we may be a little uncoordinated and paralyzed, respectively, but our thumbs are still green, and we've got that agrarian je ne sais quoi."

And so it was a little surprising when carrot tops shot from the earth in a week – with not a single lettuce sprout in sight. A month later I had concluded that the seeds were a dud. And weren't we all a little tired of silly lettuce names? Butter lettuce, indeed. Iceberg. The lettuce head that sank the Titanic. I think not. And within six weeks I had given up on the butter lettuce, grateful that I had also planted romaine. We let things go. We move on.

Though certain memories keep chasing me, and they all have to do with gardening. I was maybe seven years old when my mother sprinkled carrot seeds in a slightly raised bed rimmed by desert rocks beside our home. This was the only portion of her extensive gardens devoted to vegetable growing. The rock-bordered bed was adjacent to our front gate, right up against the harsh oleanders and splintery wooden fence that protected us from the outside world. And just across the entranceway sidewalk, with low privet hedges on one side, and that arcing, pie-shaped patch of Juniper on the other. None of these plantings were inviting, not even the irises in their sandy desert patch. But the small vegetable plot felt warmer. I dug around there with my mother, engaged and at peace. I believe my mother may have found relative moments of calm in gardening.

Left to its own devices, southern California soil hardens like a brick, a propensity the late eighteenth-century Spanish explorers found useful in building their forts and Franciscan missions. This hardening proves more problematic for a twelve-year-old, and in the autumn of 1959 things weren't going so well with me and my hoe, hacking at the ground beside my father's driveway. By then, my parents had gotten divorced, and my brother and I were living with my father in an apartment above his office. Converted from an old, once-prosperous house, the home/office was distinctly un-homey. And the only part of this that seemed changeable to my twelve-year-old mind was the grounds. The land hadn't been tilled, turned or tended for decades, and the gravel driveway felt particularly harsh. That's why I decided to create a small triangular garden, right in a spot where the two sections of driveway split. There were going to be flowers, of what type I wasn't certain, but something green and colorful. I found old sections of wooden trellis, arranged them in a triangle and hoped they wouldn't fall over. In softer soil, it would have made sense to dig a trench and sink the wooden pieces into the ground. But this was unthinkable in the hard desert clay. I devoted all my energy to hacking and picking at the pathetic ground.

I was at work in this garden triangle one Saturday when my father wandered outside. He was angry and agitated. I thought he would be pleased to see my landscaping underway, but his mind was elsewhere. He was delivering a sort of year in review. It had been the year of divorce, the year when my parents took separate trips at the Christmas school holiday, and I ended up spending the next six months with my aunt and uncle in upstate New York, theoretically a better place to be while my parents split up. Now my father stared at the hard ground. You took care yourself pretty well, he told me. You got yourself set up for a pretty cushy six months in New York while I had to battle your mother, he said. It was understood between us that we were somehow equals, he and I, me a little adult, he a big one, and battling the mother-wife was an unspoken joint endeavor.

His words cut and stung, and I protested, felt crushed and betrayed and ran inside crying. In the following weeks, I made some minor progress on the triangular garden patch, actually getting some seeds planted and growing. In retrospect, they would have grown much better in soil of the sort I now work in my raised beds here in Menlo Park. But I made do, and the flowers did their best, desert ground being always grateful for water. Within three years my father's medical practice had more or less collapsed, and we were moving to Riverside, a small city an hour from Los Angeles. We packed our possessions in boxes. The movers came. And on the final day I stood in the empty and unused lot behind our soon-to-be-abandoned house.

The place had never felt like home, but nothing did. In this, my last autumn in Banning, California, my gardening efforts had retreated to this derelict, weedy ground. I had long since given up on the triangular garden in the front of the place. Now I had a couple of withered tomato plants struggling for life. It was December, and any sensible adult would have told me to give up on tomatoes. But I didn't trust giving up. I tended the failing tomatoes the way a caveman maintained his fire. In fact, even though my father was throwing the last few things in the car, the moving van had long since departed, and I knew I would never see this place again, this strange idea came into my mind.

I would take an abandoned miniature hibachi, a tiny cast iron barbecue toy, place some charcoal in it, and light the thing. The warmth would smolder on and on and keep the tomato plants going. They would make it through the winter, heated in the way orange growers lit oil fires in the groves when a freeze threatened. I couldn't let go of the idea, even though I knew it was unrealistic, childish. I stared at the plants, staked and supported by old sections of an Erector Set. I had given up on the metal toy pieces, having outgrown them. But I had not outgrown keeping things alive, daily pouring water from a hose over the weak soil, watching the plants struggle. I wondered if the tomatoes could struggle on without me and my water and my glowing hibachi, in the dry desert cold. I got in the car and headed to Riverside.

All of which may explain why when Marlou's PET scan results came in last week I couldn't scream and shout. I wanted to, for life demands it at times, times when joy bursts forth…and something Dionysian wants to kick butt. But the PET scan isn't the whole story, or the whole story isn't completed, and the other shoe may drop. So let's be cautious and smile faintly and hope for the best. Even though this may be the best. The best ever.

Even though Avery's butter lettuce seeds, the one he ineptly released in one handful in a corner of the garden, have come to life, nine months later. A succession of crops have come and gone, including, yes, tomatoes. In fact, the entire bed has been raked and seeded with a cover crop, now shifting into warm weather growth.

Marlou's cancer cells were lingering for years, unnoticed and improbable. Just as Avery's lettuce seeds have been hanging out in the garden soil, waiting, apparently. For what? To go through a succession of mild California seasons, including the coldest weather in years. After which has come this, an early lettuce spring. With a tight clump of butter lettuce growing and crowding and jostling for garden space. It makes no sense, and it has to be seen to be believed. Or maybe it has to be believed to be seen.

Bird on the Butt

FEBRUARY 2007

Two days after returning from Hawaii there is still enough Island air dissolved in my blood to make a trip out to the planter boxes just a little confusing. The nitrogen-fixing red clover I planted there weeks ago is still largely dormant, having sprouted and more or less crossed its botanical legs, twiddling its thumbs and awaiting better growing conditions. And judging by the white frost on the neighborhood roofs, it's going to be a while before much of anything grows except moss. But not a long while. This is California, after all. Even now, it's quite warm in the sun, pleasant enough for my neighbor Buffie to come downstairs and exchange notes on the midwinter holidays. She's been there, I've been here, and her son Avery is all over the map, thundering down the stairs as only a robust four-year-old can do.

Once on the scene, Avery has questions. Avery always has questions. They are his thing. He is making sense of the world, moment by moment, and this moment is as good as any. The raised-bed planter boxes may look dormant, their cover crop barely sprouted, but Avery knows where the garden action is, more or less at his height. He's pointing and laughing at, what else, the wrought iron garden decoration Marlou gave me a few years ago. It's a thoroughly rusted silhouette of a nude woman, slightly crouched, with a bird perched on her bottom. There's a genre for these iron planter adornments, designed to accumulate rust the way bronze acquires patina. As for the design, the iron cutout depicts a slightly plump woman who seems joyously nude and at one with the bird on her rump. In spirit, it reminds me of James Thurber's drawings. Thurber women often frolicked nude, looking half bemused by their own naked pastorale. And Avery has a question. Why does the woman have a bird on her butt?

A faint chuckle from Buffie, crossing her arms and pretending to look the other way. She mutters under her breath that this happens all day long. Go ahead, she says, answer his question. I don't know what to say, and yet I do. Seated in a wheelchair I am, after all, on Avery's level. Our eyes meet. A number of things are running through my mind, one of them being that I am precisely fifteen times older than Avery. Well, I tell him, if you had a bird on your butt, wouldn't you think it was funny?

Avery laughs uproariously. A bird wouldn't land on his butt, he tells me, because birds don't like poopy places. Yes, I am on Avery's level. But I decide to get off this level by managing not to laugh and looking at the planter boxes. What shall we plant, I ask him. I stare gravely at the sprout-covered soil, then at Avery. He wants to know what the green shoots are. I tell him they are red clover, but this isn't an explanation. And the whole idea of the cover crop eludes him. Odd, for last year he saw the whole process, from the sprouting of the shoots to the growth of the stems and leaves, and then the day when gardeners went at the planter boxes with pitchforks, turning the roots into the air and ramming the green parts into the ground. He saw it, and he didn't see it. He was only three, after all. Avery is growing his own crop of ideas, insights and understandings. You never know what's going to bear harvest. But in this instance, I have scored a direct hit. Avery is matching me mood for mood, faintly scowling in concentration, such is the seriousness of our problem.

What to plant? Flowers, he says. Just like last year. No, I tell him, we need sunnier, warmer weather for zinnias. Corn, he says. I pretend to mull this over, then sadly shake my head. The nights just aren't warm enough, I say. He studies my expression. We need it to get warm, he says. That's it, I tell him – so what will grow in the cold? Aha! Spinach. Broccoli. Lettuce. Avery takes this in, then repeats it to me as though the thought is his own. Spinach should go right over there, because that's where it's going to be warm... just look at the sun. What about the lettuce, I ask him. Well, there's no room for it. Too much shade, he says. I consider this heavily, then sit bolt upright at my own insight: I wonder what's going to happen in the afternoon. I tell Avery to check on the garden sunlight after his nap and give me a full report. But he doesn't quite go for it. She's got a bird on her butt, he says. A poopy bird. Goodbye, Avery, I say, rolling my wheelchair inside. It's cold, after all.

It's also imponderable, this matter of the girl and the butt and the bird. Yet pleasant to consider, like a puzzle with no wrong answers. From this perspective, it doesn't matter if you're four or forty, or even, God forbid, sixty. The one difference is that the garden figure is a gift from Marlou. She spotted it while on vacation at Point Reyes. Which, when I think of our times there, brings me face-to-face with our days before cancer...days in the daze of summer holidays and weekends, aimless and stupefyingly enjoyable, all the pores open to sea air, Tomales Bay breezes, oysters and afternoon wine.

I recall the day Marlou bought the wrought iron silhouette woman with the bird. She had seen something, she told me, and was going to buy it for me. Hearing this, I was immediately uneasy, even downright suspicious. How could someone know me well enough to glimpse something in a store and decide, that's Paul? What was I going to have to do in exchange? What did she really want? I can't remember, but strongly suspect, that she only presented the garden ornament once we are home. Perhaps she sank the iron stick in our planter box and that was that. I recall staring at the thing in puzzlement. For one thing, it was wholly decorative. The iron piece had no other function but to adorn. And what about it was "me"? Nothing exactly, for it was more us. And more Marlou, perky and spirited and erotic.

The latter is the right word, though it has acquired the wrong meaning. The dictionary is more helpful with "eros." The Greek god of love, son of Aphrodite, progenitor of Cupid, Rome's version. Or in the language of the modern psychiatry, the sum of all life instincts. In other words, something utterly vague and indefinable, yet capable of being embodied in a flat, rusty piece of iron. A shape that is oxidizing, being returned to the earth while springing from it. A naked woman pursued by birds and literally, in the summers, bees. Sprightly, lively, not taking itself too seriously, while reveling utterly. Something Marlou wanted to give me for my garden. Which at the time, I now understand, was too much for me to easily accept. And that may be why Marlou purchased the piece as she did, on the fly, a retail snatch-and-grab, then a direct implanting in the ground. Making the piece grounded before I began to think about it unnecessarily. It was there and mine and ours. And it has taken a few years to feel what it conveys about Marlou and me and us. Why does the lady have a bird on her butt? Because she wants to be in our garden, Avery, and that's one of the rules. You have to have a bird in your butt. Understand?

It's still winter in the garden. Hard to say about the red clover and when it will finally get to work and grow. Hard to say about Marlou and her health and her future. But the hardest things to say are now saying themselves. They're speaking to me more clearly than ever. The man who built the raised beds with their wheelchair-height garden soil gave his creation one final touch. He added a metal sculpture with brackets to support a juncture of hoses. His bronze piece shows a bunch of women dancing, sheaves of wheat gathered for harvest. The piece is abstract. It is built of metal and spirit. I cannot say the same of me. Nor of Marlou. But in a miracle, I can say life's truest gift is us.

Dissolution

JULY 2008

Limbo is the place one arrives at 4:30 a.m., awake enough to not be sleeping, groggy enough to not be thinking. At least, not thinking clearly. Which is the whole point. Thinking clearly comes of sitting up, getting out of bed, sliding into the wheelchair and rolling out to another room. The latter can be any room. Just a room not named for its central piece of furniture, the bed. Try the living room. Unless you want to remain above the surface of sleep, below consciousness, in limbo.

One could say I'm a little anxious. By 11:15 a.m., I'm having an optical migraine, a transient phenomenon that alarms me. And since the thing disappears right on schedule, what really alarms me is that I'm not aware of what's alarming me. Marlou's health is always a good bet. But no, a better bet is that we are close these days, finding a lot in each other to enjoy and appreciate and laugh at. Which turns out to be one of life's most frightening experiences. It's actually easier to long for love than to find it. Finding it is like getting an all-expense-paid trip around the world, first-class, on the best airline. Only to discover that you're actually the pilot. Welcome aboard.

By 11:45 a.m., things ocular having calmed down, I roll in the time-honored path of the lost, toward Peet's. The place is jammed, Menlo Park's need for caffeine seemingly inexhaustible. Never mind, I order a double macchiato, request the thing in a cup and saucer, knowing that no tables are free. There's space at the distant counter, but I'm not going there, because I've spotted one of Menlo Park's schizophrenics ordering at the counter. I know her the way I know lots of locals. It is reassuring for me to feel part of things, greet people downtown, say hi to this one and that one. Until I realize that while I am saying hello to the one named Carol, someone on one of the moons of Jupiter is also saying hello, which explains why she isn't taking things in quite as quickly as one would expect. And just when you're wondering if she is on or off her meds, you realize she could ask you the very same question, and the answer would be no. Which is why I'm sitting in a corner, unpleasantly close to the men's room, one macchiato steaming on my lap, my lap protected by the *San Francisco Chronicle*, which since its downsizing no longer affords the thermal insulation it once did. Not to worry, for the newspaper is folded and still in its plastic suburban wrapper. A reminder to praise the universe for certain miracles.

There are more miracles across the street. Because I am dazed and demented, my actions are impulsive. Yes, I have avoided the schizophrenic Carol and am now fully caffeinated, but there's the problem of the day's schedule. I'm supposed to see Edna in her nursing home that afternoon, and when someone is pushing ninety, what the hell, no sense in postponing. So might as well have lunch in the park. I grab some take-out sushi and head for the benches. For some reason, and in my state of anxiety reason is pretty thin on the ground, I reject the benches. Never mind. There is a perfectly empty picnic table in the shade, and shade is feeling good because, as my ophthalmologist's nurse pointed out to me, bright daylight has something to do with optical migraines. And the latter have to do with things being out of control. Or, as a friend pointed out, seeing too much. I'm open to this splendid psychoanalytic interpretation, but not now. Now, I want calm. I want to sit in the dark of that redwood shade, place my sushi on the end of the empty table and ingest some food.

There's a bolt on the bottom of my wheelchair. The thing is designed to slot into an electromechanical lock, anchoring the chair while I drive. It does this quite well, perhaps too well. On even slightly uneven terrain, it drags like a ship's anchor. This condition is serious enough for me to have the bolt removed whenever I go to Europe, cobblestones being what they are. But this isn't exactly Siena, so I'm surprised when I head off the sidewalk toward the hard ground beneath the redwood tree where the picnic table shrouds itself in shadow. Surprised and not going anywhere. There's a scrape, and then there's nothing. The drag bolt has caught on the sidewalk, the chair tilting toward the ground. The tilt is enough to have one wheel spinning in the air, the other churning up dirt.

Because I am in the midst of some strange sort of internal crisis, I can't help abandoning standard practice. Part of the latter is an adaptation to one obvious condition, the breeze. The one that blows off the Bay, the one that is making this day a pleasant 72 degrees Fahrenheit, and the one that wafts things about. There's a drinking fountain next to me, dry as a bone, so it provides a convenient shelf. The logical thing would be to place the plastic package of sushi on top of the paper napkins, anchoring them against the breeze. But I seem to be exploring the anchor thing from various negative dimensions. The bolt that anchors my chair to my van is currently anchoring me to the sidewalk. The napkins that I have placed anchor-free on top of the sushi now begin to blow in all directions, as I could have predicted. And I am stuck.

Still, and one must be grateful for such things, with the defunct drinking fountain right beside me, there is something to grab. I need something to hold onto as I stand up, taking my weight off the wheelchair and trying to maneuver it half off the dirt and onto the sidewalk. This should work. But it doesn't. The anchor bolt allows the chair to spin like a top. Fortunately, this provides enough entertainment for several lunch hour regulars to rise from their benches and pull the chair to safety. I thank them all profusely. Safely on the concrete once again, I grab the sushi, note the napkins flying about and see that I am spoiling the earth. Me, Menlo Park citizen, a napkin flinger. That's my trash out there, my brown dioxin-free environmental napkins, littering the park. I am more base then base. I have no right to do this. I must fix this, now.

So, taking a slightly different route, I sail off the sidewalk – and do exactly the same thing. I am stuck again. The bolt has caught on another section of the sidewalk. Utterly unpredictable, yet in view of my state, totally predictable at the same time. I'm aware that I'm now achieving the status of, say, schizophrenic Carol. I am chronic. I am like one of those demented street people who can't remember where they live or why. This time, interestingly, the same people who helped me before do not materialize. I don't blame them. I get out of the chair a second time, knock the thing around until a young woman takes pity on me. Abandoning my lunch hour litter, I head for a shady bench. I wolf down the sushi and get hiccups. Some woman in Los Angeles had hiccups day and night for three years. This is what I'm thinking about on the way home. Sometimes being on the way home, however familiar, demands one's fullest attention.

Edna. Might as well leave now. I load myself into the van, park at Stanford shopping center across from Edna's old folks' home and remember. Shoes. I've got to find some shoes. Mine are cracked and so old that the model is no longer in manufacture. That's why God invented Macy's. The place is oddly deserted. Maybe not so odd, reports of the national economy being what they are. In the men's shoe department, I eyeball racks of the latest styles. I don't care about the latest styles. I show the woman my foot. She shows me, in the politest way, the door. Nothing in stock is going to fit my plastic brace. Why don't I try the specialty shop by Bloomingdale's? What the hell, it's all battery power, and I roll my electric wheelchair toward The Walking Shop.

There is no one inside this place, either. The shopgirl, and she is a girl, eyes me with something like suspicion. No, it is only like suspicion. Actually, it's something else. It's something that moves in an unpleasant continuum from my fears about my optical migraine to my fears about inheriting my father's brain tumor to general fears of death to a broader terror of age and dissolution. I'm not one of the beautiful people. I am not young. My aging features have sharpened, and after years of muscular imbalance my head tilts oddly on my neck. There is a reason my wheelchair is equipped with a special torso support. My body is twisting into a giant S. Viewing myself as I speed by the plate glass windows of the stores, I see the truth. I am a disabled person in a wheelchair, and my body is bending, settling and distorting under the weight of musculoskeletal time. I am losing my looks, losing any vestige of my youth, losing in general, it seems. Which may be why I seem to make this young woman uncomfortable. And I do.

This is the sort of perception I have avoided much of my life, but I'm ready for it now. Youth goes, the body goes, life goes. I am a reminder of all of these things, which may be why the twenty-something girl who has no one to wait on but me in the current retail drought looks as though she would really like to be in the storeroom, not out here fitting sportif footwear on this cripple. It's okay. She doesn't have my size. And I'm off to see Edna now. Edna will see ninety before The Walking Shop sees a size eleven-EEE. And I would rather see her.

Off

MARCH 2007

Trips, even the prospect of one trip, set my heart aflutter and send my feet a-tappin'. Metaphorically, of course. My heart valves have not fluttered in sixty years, and my feet only tap involuntarily. What I do know is that I am off to the northern counties, Sonoma and Lake, for two days of friends and hot springs. I plan to soak my body into pre-arthritic youth. I plan to soak up friends. Then return. I need to get away. There is a life out there beyond illness and treatment, and planning around illness and treatment. Marlou probably needs me to get away too, because there's a life beyond relationships. Still, my escape is a mixed blessing. A couple can get up to all sorts of things in and around the languid world of hotels and hot springs. But not us, not right now.

What I do know is that the very essence of quadriplegia has to do with immobility, and this day is all about movement. Low on tea? Forget it, because one can chart the progress of a new shipment, UPS-ing across America, from Massachusetts to Roble Avenue. They have my Visa, I have their order number, and as I set out in my wheelchair whirring and grinding through the streets of Menlo Park this morning, I am acutely aware of these vectors. Me heading north, tea heading west, Marlou heading south to chemotherapy and the gardeners hurtling toward the middle of it all.

This being the middle of spring, practically, which is to say, adjusted for global warming... it is time to turn the cover crop. Turn, turn, turn. To everything there is a pitchfork and a time. And when the gardeners turn up for their weekly blow job, not to mention sweep job and trim job, time is what they're out of. Sorry, the gardener says. He'll turn the cover crop over next week. While I would turn over in my grave to think of how bad his timing is. Worse, I have just sprinkled blood meal over both raised beds, coating the still very green waves of grain with red-black powder. The idea was to sling a bunch of nitrogen at the soon-to-decompose grasses and vetch and fava beans and red clover. An excellent idea, and all part of an unfolding process, all taking place on the very morning of my departure. Up early and out early to the local garden supply store, back and in my parking space for the garden crew to unload the steer manure. The latter being an essential component here. To review: first the blood meal to offset the nitrogen-depleting effects of plant decomposition, then with all the grassroots turned skyward, a nice covering of manure to block out sunlight, hold moisture and – soon, very soon – hold the new plants and seeds. Spring is here.

Of course, I won't be, not for the next few days. Which was why I set all these wheels in motion. Things happening in the garden. Tea on the way. Me on my way. And now there's no way much of any of this is going to happen, at least not while I am around to see it. The cover crop grasses, coated in a nice powder of dried blood, will have to grow for another week. Marlou will be here to receive the tea. While I am soaking in hot springs. It's enough to drive a person out the door to the next thing that is supposed to be happening while other things are happening. I have promises to keep, miles to go before... Marlou spots my nails. She has been preoccupied with matters of chemotherapy and its complications, such as a hacking cough, enough to distract her from her major life project of grooming me.

I roll in the door of Sky Nails, once again. And, once again, I feel like a goldfish who has just flopped into a nightclub. Are you supposed to sit at a table... order how many drinks... use a straw... go use the men's room now or later? And is there a men's room? This question underlies much of my experience at Sky Nails. Is it just me, or does a definite hush descend as I roll my wheelchair inside? Surely the womanly conversation – I am the only man – shifts gears. In any case, Helen shifts into action. I preferred Mai, my last nails practitioner. Helen is quite nice, but she has the wrong sort of name. I might adopt the name Wing Ho, and there would be nothing wrong with this. And there is nothing wrong with Helen, except that this one is far from Troy. She's from Hanoi, or thereabouts, which I think is splendid. And I think her original name is something different, but who's to quibble? Meanwhile, Helen tries to place me. Are you such-and-such's husband? Yes, I tell her, Marlou's. She nods. Mary Lou, she says. I'm thinking this is close enough. She's doubtless thinking of someone else. It doesn't matter.

Particularly since she is going at my nails with remarkable speed. Yes, she feels obliged to soak them. Not to mention cut and file and squirt the blue stuff, followed by the pink stuff. Buffing and nipping, along the way. No one else seems to be reading the San Francisco Chronicle in here. Pretty soon, I'm not reading it either, for with one functioning hand and all ten digits involved in various stages of improvement, there's nothing to do but surrender my limbs. In the final stage, Helen has a go at something approaching occupational therapy crossed with deep tissue massage. She runs her hands up and down my arms, a relaxing experience, and a mildly alarming one to notice how thin my skin is becoming. I am looking downright old, skinwise. Never mind, for I'm out the door in record time, heading for coffee, heading for the road.

Who knows where the road leads, except back here. Home. That's where I'm headed, via Sonoma, Middleville in Lake County, not to mention San Francisco. Up and down the map all to get home. Go figure. We are quite a species.

Earth Heart

MARCH 2007

If you doubt that Earthheart is just over your horizon, think again. Maybe you're confusing him with Braveheart, who has sunk below the horizon, weighted down with alcohol, bad driving and Jew hating. No, Earthheart is another matter, and all you have to know is that he's north. All good things are north, a sanguine direction shared by caribou and London and musk oxen and Seattle. Anyway, it's north, and that's why when my friend Jim and I discuss heading there for an overnight hot spring experience, that's the essential thing that feels good about it. The direction... north.

It's important to feel good about something. I don't feel good about Marlou's chemotherapy and my utter sense of helplessness, day after day, as she endures the chemical onslaught.

So, Jim's idea sounded downright attractive. Drive north to Harbin Hot Springs, an hour or so above the wine country of the Napa Valley, and decades away in every aspect. Harbin is one of those relics of the 1960s that survives, mostly transformed, but with enough authentic period flavor to remind me of my baby boomer roots in the 60s. Which in my own 60s are taking on an entirely different dimension.

Let's not go there. Let's go to Harbin Hot Springs. Of course, before we go, we have to begin spiritual preparation. Harbin is, after all, nominally a religious community, the Church of the Open Chakra, or some such, a mélange of Eastern, New Agey beliefs and practices, centered around hot waters. Which are definitely worthy of some form of worship.

Especially if you are an aging partial quadriplegic with more aches than toenails. The water runs hot out of the arid oak-and-grassland hills of southern Lake County, and the Harbin folk guide it into a series of pools. The waters must have been a healing godsend to the native tribes over the centuries. In the absence of

HBO, steaming mineral waters must have made quite an impact. They still do. Today, Harbin has its period charms, Gaudiesque railings made out of plaster, stainless steel sculpted fish spitting mineral water into pools. But the thing is run like a business, far from cheap, and attracting a new generation of beautiful people from the likes of Silicon Valley. The latter aren't very friendly, but most of the Harbin staff are.

It's important to have fond images, friendly fantasies when thinking about Harbin, because the place is quite a drive. And car trips are something I almost don't do anymore. At some point, driving began to scare me. Driving down hills in the Bay Area, even few miles from home, I've become acutely aware that the only thing pressing on the brake that stops the car is one aging, neurologically compromised, leg. Of course, one leg is enough. It is for most people, anyway. Show me a two-legged brake pusher, and I'll show you a nut. Speaking of nuts, my fear of driving, particularly losing control on hills, has begun to feed on itself. All the more important to drive somewhere, somewhere north, where everyone is naked and steaming. Harbin.

Good thing I decided to stop in Sonoma and visit my friends Gordon and Jeanette on the way.

I've known them for three decades, and they've known me through good times and bad. Since Jeanette is a fellow quadriplegic, we've seen our share of bad. And having had our share of food and wine in a homey Sonoma restaurant, it was nice to roll a couple blocks to a motel bed. I slept soundly. For the first four hours, then my eyeballs popped open at 4:30 a.m., for this is part of the preparation, the Jewish spiritual preparation. Worry. Of course, I worried about Marlou and her cancer. Then it came to me, the same way the letter came to me in the mail, arriving and wedging in a open slot in my mind. The letter from Ford. The recall letter warning me that my Ford van's cruise control has a way of bursting into flame.

No, I'm not being rhetorical. It actually catches on fire, which is why the Ford dealer in the neighboring suburb will fix my recalled van for free. If I simply drive it there, which I simply haven't. But I do remember now, this untended detail, and I can actually see what will happen, Ford flambé, hurtling around a mountain curve and right off a cliff.

At 7 a.m. in the Sonoma motel, I was up, sleepless and tending to showering and dressing. I had the television on. There's a reason God invented National Public Radio. But I had stared too long at the clock radio, trying to discern the differences between the dials and switches and the knobs and the buttons. The TV just took one click, and there it was buzzing full of middlebrow information about Iraq, cardiac diets and movie stars I have never heard of. I've never heard of anything, which was why after a morning coffee with Jeanette, the two of us whirling through the early light on Sonoma streets to her hair appointment, then time for my appointment with Harbin... I hit the road.

I hit it hard. At times, my response to what's happening with me and with Marlou and with life – is to get pissed off. I was in that mood now, angry and pounding northward, van revving, map points flying by. And as I said to Jeanette over coffee, what's the worst that can happen – I die on a road? Great. I won't know it, and if I do, maybe there's a book there. Anything to get published.

Over one steep and winding ridge, around corners and past bed-and-breakfasts into Calistoga... then up another. To pass the time, I play Bill Maher's angry political diatribes, on the radio. The perfect tone for an aggressive kick-butt drive. Sleeplessness, caffeine, anger and neurological undersupply in the bladder area conspire in an unfortunate way as I drive up the hilly road into Harbin. I rule out checking in. From the road, I can see that there's no wheelchair route into the office. I hail a passerby, an official looking one, meaning a guy with a tear drop-shaped sort of Mohawk haircut. We're very countercultural here at Harbin. We're also bursting to pee, which is why the parking complications are particularly annoying. No, I tell the guy with the haircut, I don't want to drive this van up the steep hill to the parking area, because my wheelchair won't make it down. Actually, this isn't true, but it sounds good, and what I really want to do is park close to my room. So I pull wheelchair rank, as it were, and head for a space I spotted earlier when turning my van around. Just as I begin to pull into the space, someone else grabs it.

And rather than have an urban-style honking match here in the pristine wilds, I give up. I drive around in circles, find the man pulling out and, at last, park. I hustle into the wheelchair, lower myself to the sandy ground and head for the nearest restroom. Of which there is none. There is no place to pee but in the toilet at the baths, uphill, way uphill. But, then, life is uphill, isn't it, so what is there to do but hit the joystick and hit the forty-five-degree road? The drive is so steep that I can't help but remember last week's backwards tip on a Menlo Park street. I drive cautiously, slowly, switchbacking to avoid disaster. But not quite. The toilet, by the time I reach it, requires one high step inside. A wet stain of pee descends down my trouser leg. Welcome to Harbin.

Jim arrives. Fortunate, for Harbin is a disabled accessibility nightmare. From the get-go, Jim is in charge of smoothing the way, helping me do all. The wheelchair can't get in the room, because there's a step. No one at Harbin has a clue about this, nor do they have another room. Particularly a room with a toilet, always handy for more bad moments of neurological bowel and bladder control. Never mind. We'll find a toilet elsewhere.

Meanwhile, I'm getting undressed. Off with the urine-soaked trousers. And I know just what to do. I roll to a nearby garden hose and have Jim spray my trousers. Once I decide they are adequately soaked, I look for a spot to hang them. It occurs to me that all of this pants-rinsing regularly annoys Marlou, but she's far away, and this is quickly establishing itself as guy space. That's why Jim and I spot the logical trouser-hanging location at the same time. Off the side mirror of my van. There they are, blue jeans swinging in the breeze, dripping right beside the Harbin foot traffic thoroughfare. A blue badge of urinary courage. Guy space.

Jim and I talk about women and novels and what it's like to be sixty years old; as we talk, we're all the while moving around the hot springs. I swim in the cold pool. Then I soak in the hot pool, which is steaming like a lobster pot so scalding that after a while the nude bodies of nubile young women climbing in and out of the water have little effect on me. That's because the waters are getting to me. Their effect is everything. In particular, I have this ache in my lower back, and the waters, sulfurous, with bits of algae and god-knows-what floating about, are penetrating to this pain point.

Jim suggests a massage. Harbin has a slew of bodyworkers, a virtual factory for deep tissue work, oil work, flotation treatments. I say no, then I say yes. Jim has this seductive effect. He offers playfulness, mixed with the grief of a middle-aged man, and he's an extrovert, a good balance for me. I sign up for massage. Of course, the massage will be the next day, when I'll be driving home, but never mind. For now, it's a New Agey dinner on the lower level of the Harbin buildings. To dine there, I have to abandon my wheelchair and walk down one staircase, then up another. The food is quite wonderful. And afterwards, emerging into the night, the dark rural sky is lit up like the Hayden Planetarium. Jim points out some stars. I'm grateful for Jim, for stars, and for sleep. I do a lot of the latter. And dammit if in the morning there isn't a dawn. By the time I step down from the room and into my wheelchair, a pink light is rising over the hills. A pink hand is rising over the espresso machine in the Harbin coffee bar, and I'm grateful for that too. I'm grateful for everything. This hot springs in a canyon, where there are still a couple of women wearing tie-dyes, a couple of men with hair in a bun and a creek running through dry volcanic hills. It is all, as Jim says, sweet.

After the coffees, and after the Chinese macrobiotic eggs and vegetables, naturally there's the hot springs. They've gotten hotter overnight, or I've gotten older, or both. After my first dip in the hottest pool, I have a momentary swoon on the slate bench outside. I also have a brainstorm. I ask Jim to borrow the hose from the bath attendant. He sprays me, and the cold blast revives enough of my being to submit to another boiling.

Which is the condition I find myself in when I join up with

Earthheart in the massage center. He's about my age, and he's worked there for twenty-five years. I can't believe how easily he gets me up on a very tall table. Yes I can. Jim is there to help, and after that, I'm in another world. Earthheart works over my body in a familiar way, finding the tense spots, grinding into them with his elbow. Meanwhile he keeps up a sort of New Age patter. Which is all about my trauma, how my energies got disconnected at the moment of my shooting. Of course, how well connected was I to start? He's asking this. No mincing words here. As far as he's concerned, he's dealing not with a paralyzed person, but a victim of violence. He wants to know where my limbs were when I was shot, if I fended off blows, how it hurt to be slugged in the mouth, and how I fell.

I'm getting something there, he says. He's talking about the normal spasm in my right fingers, and "getting something" to him means losing something to me. I am generally ashamed of these spasms, have taken a lifetime to conquer my self-consciousness, and now Earthheart is telling me to breathe into them. Very good, he says, we're connecting the dots, getting this in touch with that, integrating. I'm now reaching the early stage of overdose on New Age twaddle, but something holds me back.

Earthheart sees the paralysis and misalignment of my limbs not as a neuromuscular phenomenon, but as a traumatic moment frozen in time. On and on he goes, loosening my muscles, and inviting me to take part in this dialogue about the night I was shot. Which I do, although the whole thing feels invasive, but what doesn't to an introvert? Something in me isn't surprised to see this bodywork session veering toward curtailment, for the usual bladder situation is upon us. Getting off the high table and finding a restroom is going to take forever.

Pee in the rattan wastebasket, Earthheart suggests. True, it has a plastic liner. I pee without getting off the table, we resume – and for this I am indescribably grateful. For maybe this isn't the most sophisticated discussion I've ever had, but it's a healing exchange, and Earthheart has just shown himself to be as paralytically adaptive as I am. I do know this: no one has ever invited me to try to feel how I hold the aftermath of violence in my body.

Meanwhile, he keeps talking. Cringing, going rigid, ducking, these are understandable physical responses, he says. But why not consider other options? There's a way to hold my body, he tells me, a style and a physical attitude that proudly acknowledges my injury. It's all matter of fact, this therapeutic chitchat, and by the time it's over I feel something that I confess is rare in my life. I feel manly. And with that, I get dressed and drive home.

Travels

Zion

AUGUST 2006

The thing about having special needs, not to mention a special spinal cord, is that you get to feel, well, special. Like the Blue Plate Special or the Midnight Special. You're kind of featured, on sale this week only, and various other things, all of which make up for people staring and preferring that you're not in their offices forty hours per week. But in the end what life delivers is always more disappointing, not to mention ironic. So that you get a little too used to special status. Which brings us to Zion Canyon. Actually, it brings us to Las Vegas, gateway to Zion Canyon. Las Vegas thinks it is the gateway to itself. One of these days a licensed medical professional will give the city a resuscitative bitch slap, and Las Vegas will stagger out to the edge of its own desert, look for Zion, get confused, bone up on nature lore, mostly trying to remember why they call the wind Mariah. The simple answer being that the wind is not Mormon. It was the Mormons who called Zion, Zion. All you have to call is the eight hundred number for the Zion Lodge. And, yes, they have a wheelchair accessible room. And besides that, they have a wheelchair-accessible park.

Human accounts of wheelchair access vary greatly. That's because wheelchairs and wheelchair users vary greatly. Your macho paraplegic who plays two games of wheelchair basketball before breakfast, just as a warm-up to all-terrain rugby in the afternoon, will have one view of whether or not a national park trail is cripple-friendly. An able-bodied middle-aged woman pushing her not exactly weightless husband up and down geologically tilting sandstone slabs will have another. But as for hitting the trails, we're not there yet. We're not even in Zion. We're in Las Vegas, pulling out of the airport, and thinking that, sure, the place is tacky, but it does have an allure. Especially once you've seen the Eiffel Tower perched right next to the Parthenon.

And you're thinking, wow, it should always have been like this, because think of the airfares between Paris and Athens. When right here the epochs share a parking lot, and you can have a beer in one and nachos in the other. So, why not do that very thing? Just swing into Bellagio for a quick self-park, followed by a little lunch before you're on the way to the main national park event.

Within an hour you wonder what all these people are doing with their sandals and their children, wandering about dazed and talking too loud, drifting past Cartier display windows on their way to – where? After all, you were on your way to Zion and now you're here. And "here" has more places to eat then you can shake a stick at. And shaking a stick is what you would do if you were at Zion, because stick shaking is what the out-of-doors is all about. Anyway, you're here, so you might as well order Ahi tuna encrusted in something and served in a salad beside the famous Bellagio fountains, which may be on or off, though their status really doesn't matter, because you and your wife are arguing about something. The something feels terribly important, but also feels old, old as you. Because old is all you can feel when your waitress and the hostess and most of the Bellagio diners have stepped right off the runway of some fashion house. And you feel not only old, but more quadriplegic than ever.

Which is why it's a relief to be back on the interstate and hurtling toward a mountain cliff. The base of the mountain cliff, to be precise, which at the eleventh hour opens slightly to reveal a canyon, a slit just wide enough for a freeway to pass. Which you do, passing out of Nevada, pirouetting across a corner of Arizona and landing squarely in Utah. Everything in Utah is done squarely. Utah is square; just check out a map. And the thing about being squarely Utahan is that you know where you are. And where you are involves being Mormon, procreating frequently and staying pretty much out of the way of the management of Zion National Park. The latter is run by the feds, a.k.a. Department of the Interior, and the park lodge at Zion serves caffeine and alcoholic drinks, though not without a few restrictions. Never mind. This is the first thing you'll check out as soon as you get to the lodge. But, remember, we're not there yet.

We are at the visitor center. All national parks have a visitor center. Why? Because visitors need a center. Americans are not a very centered people these days, having been knocked badly off kilter by 9/11, so they congregate at visitor centers hoping to get concentric. Many of them do. We did. A quick look at the map, a glance at the rules, and the Zion experience begins to make a kind of sense. Only one thing about Zion. You can't drive. In fact, even to take your car from the park entrance to the lodge requires a large red card, mounted in your windshield, which the park ranger hands you while making you swear, scout's honor, that you absolutely will not wander about the park in your car. In fact, you're going to leave your car at the lodge, and more less forget it. Or the Rangers will get you. Got it? As for getting around, that's what the park shuttles are for. They are small articulated buses, powered by natural gas and virtually silent. They run every five minutes or so and, yes, they are wheelchair accessible.

Which puts the battle-hardened quadriplegic in something of a quandary. For the dirty little secret of disabled life is that there are benefits. First boarding the airplane. Free admission to the Musée d'Orsay. That sort of thing. So it's natural, almost instinctive, to do what that large woman with the disabled scooter is currently doing with the ranger – getting special dispensation. She wants to drive her car, claims the scooter won't make it on the shuttle's wheelchair lift. Listening to this, I know better, or think I do. In any case, I would demand a trial run. I think the ranger should adopt a show-me stance and insist that the woman give the lift a try. As for me, well I'm such a unique and neurologically complex victim of the world that I really shouldn't be using the silly shuttles either. I mean, does equal access mean, you know, equality? I don't know. I don't know anything except that I'm glad I'm here, and after a few minutes driving up the canyon it's easy to see why.

Zion Canyon opens like a magical book with strata for pages. It winds like the river that made it, the aptly named Virgin River. But any observation begins to falter as the sheer walls, the vertical sandstone faces, ascend to where they started. Up there. Way up there. At a point so high, descending into a canyon so narrow, that the canyon walls don't seem so much to wind as to stagger. Zion Canyon doesn't look as though it's going to hold together much longer, that the whole plunging earth-tone vastness of it will give way. Within the next twenty million years or so. Meanwhile, here it is, alternately purple and red, microscopic pine trees dotting the top rim, big aspens here below, where the Zion Lodge provides benches for its carless patrons. A good place to sit for hours and hours and wonder how anything could get so big and high and sandstone and geologic, while on the lawn in front of the lodge screaming three-year-olds chase the occasional wild turkey. No, not the whiskey, the bird.

The June morning feels mild, almost brisk. The lodge and its lawns feel shadowy. They are. The sun glares off the red sandstone summits, thousands of feet above, but here it's all purple morning shadows. Which, as anyone will tell you, is good. No sense in waiting for the day, which in June brings shimmering waves of heat stroke. The park rangers are up and at it early on a summer day. They urge visitors on with 9 a.m. hikes, 10 a.m. lectures and 11 a.m. bus tours. So, we board an 8:45 a.m. shuttle and head up the canyon. The wheelchair lift works smoothly. The driver even knows how to run it. Zion Canyon's main road, now shut to everything except the shuttles, feels like a wide mountain trail with big rest areas. The latter are the shuttle stops, each with its own stone shelter and informative signs. The last stop, at the head of the canyon, leads to a trail through the red narrows, where the mile-high canyon walls close in to twenty feet apart. My wife pushes the wheelchair, a folding, non-battery-powered thing. We bounce and tilt over stones and ruts, keeping pace with the ranger and her acolytes, mostly middle-aged women. It's a slow group, so I don't slow it down. We stop to look at plants and oddities of the sandstone canyon walls. Water oozes here and there. The appearance of water in a place so arid seems miraculous, especially when it arrives sideways, coming laterally out of cooperative strata. The ranger says it takes many centuries for rain to percolate through the surface ground, down to where we're standing, on a trail beside a glistening rocky face. Amid the glistening there are black dots, bumps, and they are snails, a species unique to Zion Canyon. Around them grow ferns and vines and other water-loving plants, a curious garden hanging off a stone face, which keeps cool in the evaporative air. The humidity borders on zero, and everyone keeps telling you to drink water.

There are lots of people on the trail, and on the way back, at the shuttle stop several pitch in and help the wheelchair pusher. My wife isn't too keen. She would prefer to do this herself, but she has over time accepted that we depend on the kindness of strangers. At the shuttle bus stop we depend on the wheelchair lift, which works beautifully every time. We head down the canyon to the visitor center and hang out in the heat. The latter drives us back to our room. Well, not exactly, for it's the shuttle that drives us. And it's the shuttle that around 6 p.m., when the valley again descends into shadow, a layer of white sandstone reflecting the sun in natural indirect lighting, drives us back up the same road we took in the morning. We ask the shuttle driver to stop at Big Bend. That's what it is, a point where the canyon turns, all thousands of feet of it, a deep crook cut by a shallow creek. The shuttle purrs away, leaving us alone. Which is the odd thing about this major national park destination, with its throngs of sightseers. Without cars rumbling up and down the road, the occasional hiker seems like nothing, and the canyon vastness seems like an echoing wonder. My wife starts pushing the wheelchair down the road. It's easy. The road is paved, the next shuttle is minutes away, and we are alone in Zion. We stop and get another angle on the bend and some of the features the shuttle drivers point out. There's the zigzag trail high on the opposite face of the canyon. Here's the wooden tower that once held up steel cables to slide logs from the forested summit down to the valley floor. Maybe those logs now comprise the benches and joists of the lodge. It's an easy, utterly quiet moment of canyon solitude. We could have insisted on driving, but we would have missed this. There's no missing the next shuttle, for they run every few minutes. We deliberately miss a succession of them. With the departure of each, the place becomes ours again. In quadriplegic terms, it's a true wilderness experience, empty and alone, yet safe. Mother nature is a fearsome thing. And human nature can be the same. But not at this moment, which has given high meaning to access and lift.

Unified Field

NOVEMBER 2007

Einstein spent his life trying to develop the unified field theory of disabled travel, and although he failed, we still have this: $DT = CC / €10002$. In this famous equation, however imperfect, disabled travel (DT) is represented as a function of the calorie constant (CC) in relation to the value of the Euro squared. To demonstrate the underlying principles, the disabled Europe-bound traveler can perform several simple experiments at (or near) home. Such an exercise is essential, as well as illuminating.

Let's start at the end of the equation, because this is where the math is easiest. Think of the Euro as a playground kid. In fact, he is the childhood chum at the end of the teeter-totter, a.k.a. the seesaw. Yes, these once standard and timeless items of playground equipment have fallen out of favor. Allegedly too many kids have fallen off of seesaws. Never mind. There is still a teeter-totter around somewhere, and imagine it. Imagine you are on one end and the Euro is on the other. Be sure to choose a moment when the financial markets enable the Euro to go up and the dollar to go down. You love your descent. You laugh as the Euro is flung upward and you and your currency drop downward. Ha ha.

In fact, to really revel in this experience and fully prepare yourself for European travel, do what I did. Go into downtown Menlo Park, take several thousand dollars out of your bank account, go into the park across the street from Peet's Coffee and pull out some matches. First, light a fifty-dollar bill. Everyone will marvel. Go across the street and have a latte, then return to the park and light a one-hundred-dollar bill. Your neighborly coffee drinkers will applaud. Ready for that thousand-dollar bill? Go for it. Have a triple latte, whip out the matches and light up. You'll be glad you did it. Because lighting up lightens up the burden of turning on the nightly BBC Business Report and watching the value of American dollars plummet. After all, you're spending a lot of them every day, many more than you want to know. Thus, the Euro part of the equation.

The Calorie Constant is much easier to understand. It's three thousand. No matter what you do, no matter where you go, every day, everywhere, you will eat three thousand calories. You can talk about lightening up. You can gaze bewildered at those trousers you let out just before you set off in your travels. You can do anything, but the Calorie Constant is always just that: Constant, three thousand. It doesn't matter whether you are aboard the *Queen Mary* 2, or in Gloucestershire cheese country, London curry land or Provence. Three thousand.

Next, consider the unknowns. This part drove Einstein nuts. He tried pulling out his hair. Then he pulled out all the stops. Then he pulled out of a bridge tournament, his membership in the local Rotary Club and a course in do-it-yourself hairstyling. Nothing worked. There were still unknowns that could not be accounted for and, as a result, Einstein spent his last years wandering around Princeton wondering if he should take up golf. In the end, he settled on miniature golf. The course was easier to conceive of at once, there was a windmill moving at a constant speed and, if you missed a putt, gravity would take over. Gravity was very important to Einstein.

Chance, unknowns, uncertainties, random events, fortune, fate. Want to see these factors at work? Let's go back home, to Menlo Park, California, sit down in front of a computer screen and take a long, hard and, yes, virtual, look at Aix-en-Provence, France. Why are we looking? Because we have had this simple spatial problem staring us hard in the face. The marvel that is known as the TGV, the world's most stunning and more or less fastest train, requires extremely straight tracks, and there's no way a railway line of this speed and import is going to hang a sudden left just to stop at a has-been provincial capital. No way. Okay, it will stop, but on the outskirts of Aix-en-Provence. About five miles out of town. And the problem? There's a bus into town, but according to the website for the local transit agency, the Aix-en-Provence tourist information office and God himself, this bus doesn't take wheelchairs. Five miles is a long way from your hotel room on a cold November night, and a railway station – even a high-speed one – is no place to sleep. That's why you have wracked your brain, stayed up nights late, had your wife phone France several times and hired a chauffeur with a special lift-equipped van to transport you (and, as the driver bragged, up to four cripples total) to your hotel room.

Of course, our driver wasn't there – but miraculously it was no big deal to rent a Renault Kangoo, a van favored by Provençal plumbers and, in the future, all California cripples. And as discussed earlier on this book, problem solved. Actually, the final, ultimate problem was solved the following morning at the French equivalent of Home Depot. There Marlou ordered the most helpful staff to cut a piece of authentic Provençal pine, grown in Norway, to a five-foot length and two-and-a-half-foot width, which cost us the modest sum of ninety dollars, approximately (see the above Euro seesaw principle for a fuller explanation). This *planche* (plank) served quite nicely to get my electric wheelchair in and out of the high-ceilinged Kangoo van. As for our special chauffeur with his van for four cripples, forget it. We sent him on his Provençal way.

What did this prove? It proved that now that the weather had turned nasty, balmy Mediterranean days over and the more sinister mistral now blowing its way from the Alps, we no longer had plans. Yes, we had a map. But so did Einstein. Did that help him? Don't bet on it. Bet on four-wheeling with Marlou around the town of Saint-Rémy. Remember, this is where Vincent van

Gogh was hospitalized. We were, for the usual perverse touristic reasons, going to see this site of his clinical trials.

But something had gotten into my wife. We were taking what might be euphemistically described as back roads. We were on the outskirts of the byways of the periphery of the unmarked portions of semi-abandoned tracks that were not designed for tourists and, in fact, not on any map, existing solely for goatherds, agricultural workers and small-time olive thieves. The roads were barely one lane wide, deeply rutted, exceeding forty-five degrees in steepness. And, at one desperate point, we found ourselves not only lost (Marlou had not mentioned the "L" word, but we were) and actually slipping backwards down a hill, tires spinning gravel. While my wife burned rubber, engine revving, spirits soaring, because, fuck it, we were traveling. And we knew it, both of us, and there was no destination and there was no purpose and, trust me, there was no deadline.

Which explains why, without going to see the famous Roman aqueduct up the highway, we decided to park in the magical disabled space that appeared in the center of town. A sign warned nondisabled drivers to "take my space if you want to take my disability." We warmed to this sentiment. Marlou spotted a restaurant beside the parking space. That looks nice, she said. No it doesn't, I said. I knew what was happening – she was getting cold feet. And why not? It takes nerve to back the electric wheelchair down the planche, all on her own, while I, the disabled husband, look on.

But it also takes nerve to patch out and spin rubber in van Gogh's back streets. So, it didn't take much encouragement to get Marlou out of the car, the wheelchair on the ground, and the two of us wandering the magical lanes, alleys and streets barely wide enough for a car. A provincial French market town, but a rich one, full of specialty shops for olive oil, linens, spices and, naturally, artworks. Of course, we were having a minor fight within seconds. Marlou accused me of dinking around while the luncheon clock ticked away, and her blood sugar lowered. I counter-accused.

Then we both saw it. La Maison Jaune. Any restaurant that can afford to have the entire downstairs of an eighteenth-century townhouse devoted entirely to lobby space is making a bold statement, isn't it? Naturally, there was no way up the sidewalk, no way in the front door, and the eating area was only accessible via an enormous flight of stairs. A flight of fancy, lunch in such a place? Absolutely not. This is why God invented batteries. This is why God invented Marlou. With power, and faith and the kindness of Provençal strangers, we were over the doorsill, rolling my wheelchair into the dark recesses of the coatroom and ascending the steps to one of the most delightful – and most expensive – lunches I have ever had. How did it happen? Ask Einstein.

Shropshire Lad

NOVEMBER 2007

When my English relatives, really German Jews, began touring me about in my early years in London, much of what I saw left me unimpressed. Imagine, an entire village intact in the Kent countryside and open to inspection by tourists like me. Just imagine. I tried hard to imagine, but I was mostly imagining what it would have been like to be not only physically intact, but emotionally so, confident, open and able to enjoy the weekends on my own. Instead of driving about the Home Counties with people my parents' age. As for the villages, churches, pubs, museums and other touristic manifestations, all I could be was polite. I could not really tell the difference between a village restored by the National Trust and one constructed on the hard clay of Anaheim by Walt Disney.

Let's have some tea, I would generally suggest. Tea meant cakes and cream. It also meant the tea itself, caffeine being welcome to a depressed person, not to mention diuretic. Thus, tea meant looking for toilets, a task undertaken briskly and aggressively by Wilhelm, married to my father's cousin. Toilets were usually found in pubs, where astonished publicans found Wilhelm at their door clearing the path for me with the helpful observation that there was a cripple in his car. In short, there was a lot of emotional drama, mostly internalized, attached to my first impressions of Britain.

Which makes it so pleasant to travel around Shropshire, where Marlou has recently gone searching for ancestors. The beauty of England is more muted and subtle than, say, Yosemite or the Grand Canyon. It is also ideal for a quadriplegic, a person whose world is naturally small, whose journeys are short and confines are narrow. It did my heart good to see a railway station functioning in one particular Shropshire village. Buxton. One of Marlou's nineteenth-century forebears hung out here at one point, and I was prepared to do the same. The rise of gentle hills, the village nestling in a valley, a short and, doubtless, empty train making its diesel way once or twice a day to the station by the pub... I could get used to this. No one commutes to London from Shropshire, at least not this part, for the distance is too great. People live here. I don't know how they make a living, but it's someone's world. And I could imagine it as mine. The surrounding slopes are forested, and when one is traveling by car the trees appear and then disappear just as quickly. But traveling around Buxton, Shropshire, by wheelchair, nothing would disappear. Except the sun, of course. But if one can live with that... and in four years of English weather I discovered that I could... the rest isn't a problem. In Buxton, I could stare out the window on cold days, sit in the shade of the churchyard on hot ones and, when desperation got the better of me, go to the railway station and watch a train rumble by. England is a small place full of small pleasures, and so is quadriplegia. We spent less than half an hour in Buxton, such was our itinerary. But I got the idea.

England's army was in ruins after the Battle of Agincourt, but it didn't matter with young Henry on the throne. Which is why one shouldn't worry about the Royal Shakespeare Company, now lying in ruins beside the River Avon. While the troupe's new theater is under construction, plays run on a temporary stage nearby. "Temporary" doesn't do the new venue justice. It's a tiered, thrust-stage auditorium that looks much like the new permanent version will look. In any case, *Henry V* roared to life upon it, with all the flair and articulation that makes the company justifiably famous. This one wasn't a modern staging, that is to say, not a production in modern dress. But that's not really the point. The Royal Shakespeare Company always teases the modern meaning out of its works.

How chilling to watch the heroic British slitting the throats of their captured French prisoners. It's only a moment in an epic plot, but there's no avoiding it. Shakespeare wrote in an era when power and its privileges, war and its necessities, life itself, were all regarded with a different set of values. The play made me think of my own unheroic life. I seem to do everything with maximum caution. In Henry's world, there is little room for caution and even less time. No one ruminates; everyone knows what they have to do, and fate falls as it falls. I don't want to fall myself, particularly on my cousin's stairs. Which is why I pick my quadriplegic way through life gingerly. This does, I suppose, make it possible for me to travel across several countries, navigate the upstairs of my cousin's Gloucestershire home and generally burn through thousands of tourist dollars without incident. As for heroics, mine is a different world and, upon consideration, maybe I need a different definition.

Queenly

NOVEMBER 2007

The supreme shipboard moment, long imagined and never even close to experienced, looked very much like a chaise lounge, with me in it, staring at the open sea, waiters stopping by now and then to freshen my tea, add an extra blanket to my lap or generally inquire after my good health and well-being. And oddly, this moment never occurred aboard the *Queen Mary 2*.

We came close, Marlou and I, to this sort of thing on the next-to-last day. We had gone out on the deck, which is to say deck number seven, the one that circumnavigates the entire ship, giving joggers a good third of a mile. Actually, giving them considerably more, when one considers the wind resistance. Built for the crossing of vast seas with fierce waves and battering breezes, the *Queen Mary 2* easily adds its own nautical speed to that of an onrushing wind. The effect on deck certainly gives pause to a rolling quadriplegic. I have never felt that my one-hundred-sixty pounds, combined with my wheelchair's two hundred, could be slowed by wind. But out on the deck, on that final Wednesday, the Atlantic breezes were blowing me backwards, or so it seemed. The air was only about 62 degrees, but the wind made it feel like 40.

Reaching a favorite exercise spot on deck, I lifted myself to walk a few feet around an enclosed area where sturdy handrails made for a natural physiotherapy session. I only got a few yards down the railing before turning back, body shivering, balance faltering, for the breeze was fluttering my pant legs like sails. These conditions squelched my one shot at deck sitting, tea sipping, ocean staring. There was too much breeze, although waiters kept coming by with hot mugs of consommé and there was every opportunity to do the deck chair thing. But, inexplicably in almost a week aboard, there was too little time.

We had been at sea for a full day and a half when I discovered that the journey could be viewed on Channel 38 of our cabin's television. A succession of screens displayed wind , temperature, ship's speed, miles elapsed, miles to go, while a thick red line showed our progress across the Atlantic. "Honey, how come we're only at Newfoundland?" I asked Marlou. She stared at me. "Paul, it's a ship."

Good point. There's a reason Virgin Airways doesn't go thirty mph and the *Queen Mary 2* does. And because a ship moves slowly, passengers should get a chance to slow down. But this was not the case. In fact, being aboard the ship proved downright adrenal, high on frenzy, short on sleep. It's not just that there were so many activities, although there were – each day dawned with a six-page listing of lectures, concerts, plays, films, nautical instruction, cooking classes, book groups and miscellaneous sessions. No, it's the inspiring nature of the ship itself. It's arguably the world's largest ship, and, arguments aside, the most powerful. Go to the observation deck behind the bridge. Or take the outside elevator to, say, the bar one level down, or the library several levels down, and take a high, wide look at the ever disappearing North Atlantic. This crossing (no, it's not a cruise) included a first-time screening of a British documentary on the Apollo missions to the moon in the late 1960s and early 1970s. The film is all about daring, imagination and lofty goals. So is the QM2.

High spirits on the high seas. Evenings in which music emanates from at least ten distinct lounges, restaurants and theaters. Some of the best music is on a smaller scale, with the feel of a good evening of piano jazz at the Algonquin Hotel in New York. Class acts. In many ways the ship is a class act itself. Actually, the walkways are like a Cunard museum, with photos and text giving us endless perspectives on the history of passenger steamships. Immigration, dining on board, life below decks, famous people who have sailed, caring for pets on board, navigation. In short, the ship seems very conscious of its past. Sometimes this is a problem.

The interior decor has a jumped-up Art Deco feel about it. Much of the time this works. Some of the time, it doesn't. The ship's cinema is most impressive, with aisles and entranceways lined with statuary and decorations that suggest the 1930s but work perfectly well in 2007. Of course, the fact that there is a film theater at all astonishes me. Sailing, sailing. That's happening, moving over the ocean blue, while one sits and watches a film in total oblivion. The same is true of the Royal Court Theatre, adjacent, although the name makes me cringe. The original one in Sloane Square, London, is so associated with playwrights such as John Osborne that I kept shaking my head in disbelief at the Ukrainian dancers doing Broadway routines with wireless microphones strapped to their heads – that's what transpires in the *Queen Mary 2*'s Royal Court. Actually, it's a remarkable thrust-stage venue for all kinds of performing artists, from the ship's Polish string quartet to recent graduates of London's Royal Academy of Dramatic Art, who actually performed abbreviated plays. *A Midsummer Night's Dream* in fifty-five minutes. *Great Expectations* in an hour-long version, which, my own expectations being low, I missed. But I had a go at a couple of the stage shows, the ship's band blaring in the background. Spotlights, a revolving stage, ever-changing scenery. The production values are high, the Ukrainians' spirits are higher. And the wages are low, throughout the ship, which did not give me a terribly good feeling.

Wretched excess. Meal after meal with impeccable service, reasonably good – certainly beautifully presented – food, cabins cleaned and beds turned down, all toilets aboard mopped and polished several times a day. And all this work is done by Filipinos, Eastern Europeans and other poorly paid hard-working people. It's not just that they do the work, but that one is encouraged to forget about it. We're supposed to be dining and sailing and gorging. But for me, it was hard to forget about all the people working. Marlou and I gave our cabin attendant and dining room waiter an extra tip. I felt good about that. The very act kept me conscious.

After all, who were we aboard the *Queen Mary 2* but a bunch of middle-class people donning tuxedos and evening gowns to play at a life none of us really possessed? The dinner table conversation ran to cruises we have known and places we have sailed. Which got boring. And things did not improve on the last night of formal dining, when the kitchen staff went on a march. I guess this is some sort of shipboard tradition. Scores of chefs in chef hats, seventy-two waiters and an additional seventy-two busboys, not to mention assorted sous chefs actually went on a procession from the lower level of the dining room, up the sweeping staircase to the second level, and marching on to the third. Why? The reasons are unclear, and the effect was somewhat stupefying. I'd been dining on the likes of pate of partridge liver for days, gotten used to plates that arrived with sauces dribbled in colored patterns, and didn't really need to have a procession of cooks or Meistersingers or anyone at all rolling past my table.

What I needed was the library. With windows cut into the ship's slanting bow that provided an overhanging view of the North Atlantic, it was one of the most exquisite book rooms I've ever seen. In fact, the library – with almost ten thousand books – would have been the perfect refuge aboard the ship, if the place had been quiet. Unfortunately, non-readers were always strolling in to have a look, people were struggling with the operation of the ship's personal computers, and the general noise level was persistent. What to do but head back to the room? Except that there were all these activities. Who wanted to miss an afternoon lecture? Or a concert? Who wanted to just sit on the balcony of our room and watch the Atlantic roll by?

I wanted to before I boarded, and now, after I'm on dry land. At the time the ship seemed to demand exploration, and that's what Marlou and I did. As though driven by unseen forces, from dawn to dusk we went about meandering. Marlou claims she doesn't like exercise, but aboard the *Queen Mary 2*, she walked miles happily and without comment. We discovered that lunch in the coffee bar was of manageable size, enjoyed in wood-paneled elegance and provided something bordering on a break. This was about the only break we got. We went and went, rolled and rolled up one deck, down another, then out another.

Because even when the entertainment wasn't interesting, the wheelchair-friendly ship was. It was even possible to stand in an observation space behind the bridge and observe the navigation, steering and general management of the vast ocean liner. It was also possible to roll a few feet out onto an adjoining deck that projected sideways, out from the hull – the flying bridge – and gaze forward into the onrushing Atlantic and backward along the ship's length... the equivalent of four football fields. Sailing, sailing. I never got used to it, never forgot it. We were in the middle of the ocean, the largest thing on the planet, the thing that engenders life and frequently claims it. The ship's captain let us know when we were passing close to the wreckage of the *Titanic*. Much was made of safety, the usual lifeboat drill, and frequent reminders that, for all the onboard folderol, cold water and silent depths were never far. I liked that. A reminder to me: It was a miracle to be crossing a vast ocean and simultaneously criticizing the tacky look of the proscenium arch in the ship's theater.

As for formal dining, two evenings surrounded by dinner jackets and evening gowns passed without incident. I was glad that I didn't bother renting a tuxedo. Nothing about the shipboard crowd seemed to warrant the bother or expense. Black bow tie, white shirt and black suit jacket did fine for me. Still, something about the feverish excitement of being on board hummed like a guitar string long after the waiter had brought the absolute last post-dessert chocolate, coffee was done and our tablemates had fled. We fled too. Our suburban lives in Menlo Park are so routine and stodgy that getting home from chorus practice at 10 p.m. feels like a wild night, what with the tooth-brushing and teakettle filling before going to bed. But here, high spirits upon the high seas, Marlou and I headed straight for the ballroom. In fact, earlier Marlou had even participated in cha-cha lessons. A dancing partner? The ship has a professional retinue on board, the "gentlemen escorts," ten or so elderly men in white jackets whose job it is to dance with the many single, and frequently older, women passengers.

While the band played vintage material from Tommy Dorsey to Sting, Marlou and I found a table at the edge of the dance floor. I knew what I had to do. I knew this black-and-white evening meant a lot to Marlou. And in some different way, it mattered to me. Just that we were here, alive and together. And it had taken sixty years for me to get here, and something similar could be said of everyone else. Marlou didn't need a gentleman escort right now, for I could stand up from my wheelchair, hold her in my arms and dance the dance of the paralyzed. The latter involves rocking back and forth, swaying with the music and keeping the backs of my thighs in fairly constant contact with the edge of the wheelchair cushion, just for neuromuscular orientation. The ship was swaying too, very slightly, and one needed to be careful. But not too careful. Not too full of care about who was watching and whether or not I made a quadriplegic spectacle of myself... pathetic in my efforts... grotesque in my failings. So, that sort of care would have to go away. What I cared about right then was Marlou, and me and Marlou, us, the couple. And we deserved a dance. So, I was up and swaying and part of the dance floor action, and I had no capacity for the cha-cha and I had no regrets.

Good to hear from the liner's third officers the next morning, giving a presentation on the technical virtues of the *Queen Mary 2*. The thing has a double-strength hull, fifty percent more engine power than any other passenger ship afloat, and most impressive stabilizers. The latter function like ailerons on an aircraft, controlled by gyroscopes and instantly responding to the slightest rocking and tilting. When the ship tilted, they did the same, turning up or down to compensate. They produced the faint fluttering vibration that emanated from deep in the ship, hundreds of feet beneath our cabin. This subtle shuddering, easily ignored most of the day, lulled me to sleep at night. It reminded me of where we were, of the ancestors that had given their lives to make all this possible, this art of navigating the planet's waters.

There was metal humming deep in the water, keeping us upright and stable. There was a man in the adjacent cabin who, in service of the Hastings Fire Brigade, had been stabbed in the eye, then contracted amyotrophic lateral sclerosis. We sat in the ship's pub (of course there was one) side-by-side, our wives across from us, comparing stories. He was, in many ways, the best reminder of all. That this is life, that it is a voyage, that the essential conditions are rough, and that it all ends.

When the end came, at Southampton, I never saw it. The ship docked, swiveling its 360-degree rotating screws to maneuver into port in the dead of night. The *Queen Mary 2* does not require tugboats. It slips into port, and we slipped off. A short cab ride to the railway station, an hour into London, and within minutes we were in another pub, this time on dry land, eating chicken tikka with Bloomsbury's lunch hour crowd. And inwardly shaking our heads and reeling in utter disbelief.

Things Work Out

NOVEMBER 2007

When anyone proudly asserts that "there will always be an England," they are probably not talking about Tottenham Court Road. London is London, and then there's all the rest. The English countryside exerts such a powerful pull and in many ways represents the true wealth of the nation – that our departure could not have been delayed any other way. Partridge death.

There we were saying our goodbyes, Marlou and me, Alistair and Caroline, as the news gradually drifted in. The trains weren't running. This confirmed everything my cousin Caroline tends to believe about the British railways. But I take the opposite view. The railways are in a transitional state. They were not always as we see them now, and in the future they will be much improved. For now, we have to take the good with the bad. This was what one of Caroline's Moreton-in-Marsh neighbors tried to explain in the railway station car park. It's the partridges. A locomotive had plowed into a flock of partridges, sucked masses of feathers into its air intake and expired. Don't blame First Great Western railway. There's a reason they are first and great.

Thus our delayed arrival in London. On the way, Caroline gave us a quick tour of Oxford. I have barely seen the place, and it's on my list. Next time. We cruised past the Ashmolean Museum, glimpsed bits of the center. We will be back. Meanwhile, we were soon back in London. In fact, we were back at the Bloomsbury Holiday Inn. And then we were wandering down Southampton Row in search of a curry.

We each have a place in which we are always strangers and always at home, and for me that place is London. I don't recognize the place. The streets are full of accents that I cannot place, the shops have changed, and I would not want to be the elderly man leaning on his cane and looking bewildered amidst the waves of young people washing in and out of the Russell Square tube station. Or would I? He looked all alone, utterly lost in this ever-changing city. But this might have been a fleeting impression. He might have family, friends, social service people to keep an eye on him, and all the essentials of a perfectly decent urban life. Besides, I am much like that man myself. I am older, move slowly and now rely heavily on others for many essentials of my life. His existence is much like my own.

I fear sleep. On some nights, I'm afraid to let go and give myself over to it. Perhaps I fear I will never wake up. Perhaps I fear the loss of control. In any case, at some point around one in the morning in London, I found myself awake. Yes, our alarm was set to go off at 4 a.m. Yes, the hotel's automated wake-up call was scheduled for that hour. No, I would count on neither, and so I stared at the ceiling for almost three hours until, at four in the morning, I was up and about. And shortly after 5 a.m. I found myself at Waterloo Station staring at a twenty-two-pound cab fare. How could it cost so much to go a couple of miles? An itemized receipt explained it all. At that hour, for a man who needed reliable transport for his wheelchair, the only solution was a radio cab. Six pounds for the reservation. Three pounds for the booking fee. A few more pounds for the fact of being a radio cab, and there we were, in front of the Eurostar terminal, looking for a porter.

It's all very modern, Eurostar, which explains why there are no porters and, also, why it took Marlou several minutes and the assistance of our cab driver to work through the intricacies of a coin-operated baggage cart. We set off, wheelchair whirring and baggage cart grinding, in search of our train. Marlou was looking worried. We had a minor tiff at the French immigration kiosk. I proceeded down one queue, Marlou took another, and by the time we were on the other side staring at the Eurostar waiting room, a sober and contentious tone had settled over the travel day. It was barely 6 a.m., and our train was still an hour away. We were not happy with each other. We were not happy with the day's trip, and the latter had not even begun.

What got us right? The short answer is years of hard work. It has taken me this long to understand that when Marlou is bossy and anxious she is still Marlou. I don't have to mount an all-out nuclear attack. I can ensure my survival as a male with, let us say, a conventional strike. And sometimes, I can even suspend hostilities. As I say, it's taken a while. On this occasion, with Marlou seated by the entrance to gate number twenty-three, bags at her side, bags under her eyes, I even managed that most chivalrous move. I went in search of a latte.

There's no doubt: life is much better caffeinated. As for me, I could wait for breakfast aboard Eurostar. Nothing to do but find an accessible toilet. This wasn't difficult. There was one with a wheelchair symbol close at hand. Unfortunately, everything inside was close at hand. The sink, the door, the toilet, the walls. I had to remove the footrests to turn my wheelchair around and get the door open.

Eurostar is, of course, one of the modern world's great wonders. Flashing across Kent, dashing under the English Channel, and hurtling toward Lille, there was barely time to enjoy coffee, decompress from the morning's anxieties and enjoy some eggs. Marlou and I had a chat. She feels that nothing must go wrong while we travel, that she must be on top of all challenges, never taken by surprise, never baffled by the procedures and devices of modern transport. In short, she was raised to be perfect. So was I. Thus, our marriage. Perfection, I told her, was asking a bit much of a quadriplegic and a cancer survivor. We were facing great challenges. Together. What more could one say?

Lille is an anonymous place in terms of train travel, a modern station and as far as one can go in northern France without being in Belgium. Which is why we spent a pleasant half hour in the company of a Belgian tour organizer and, for want of better words, missionary. King Leopold may have not done much good for the Congo, but this man has. He has run safaris and plowed his profits into a sort of a rescue mission for abandoned African girls. He showed us a photo of his African family. Marlou recognized the tribe. She also recognized me, I recognized her, and by now, fueled by coffee and inspired by this Belgian ex-army-officer-turned-one-man-NGO, we recognized our mission: getting to Aix-en-Provence in good spirits.

It was almost seven hundred miles from Lille to our TGV station in Provence. Just look at the map. Do the math. Do whatever you like, but the whole experience still will not add up. I caught a vague intimation of the *Trains à Grande Vitesse* thing on the platform as another train pulled in from somewhere. The electric motors roared. One expects a diesel engine to make noise, but not the mere motor, the sum of copper windings that actually drive the wheels. As I say, this motor roared. And soon we roared with it, or with its TGV cousin.

I always feel I'm going fast at eighty mph on the Amtrak straightaway that is west of Sacramento, but moments out of Lille we were going twice that. Which meant that forty-five minutes later we were pulling out of the train station at Charles De Gaulle Airport, Paris. And fifteen minutes after that, already in Burgundy. Our train flipped into hyper-drive and we hurtled south at something much closer to two hundred miles an hour. So, do the math, and don't be surprised when Aix-en-Provence rolls into view after only four hours.

We were met at the station by two attendants who took us to the curb, where we awaited Monsieur Bertrand. Who is he? Marlou's own answer to the Aix-en-Provence TGV station wheelchair problem. There is no accessible transport from the station to the town – I had spent hours researching this problem on the Internet. So we had found this man, Bertrand, who runs a sort of medi-van service for local people in wheelchairs. Marlou had called him weeks ago on and discussed a pickup at the train station.

We waited and waited in front of the TGV station, but Monsieur Bertrand didn't turn up, so Marlou phoned him. He was in Nice and not expecting us. Marlou, he insisted, was supposed to call and confirm. Marlou had been talking about calling for days, but she kept putting the phone call off. Making oneself understood by phone in a foreign language is a daunting experience. She kept avoiding the call, and now here we were, stuck without a ride.

Except, that we weren't stuck. I knew we weren't. Perhaps, for the first time in my life, I knew things were going to work out, because they were going to work out. I wasn't going to berate Marlou, because that is how both of us have been raised, and more criticism is coals to Newcastle. Besides, something was going to happen. And it wasn't going to be bad. I couldn't help but remember my quadriplegic friend Jeanette who, stuck at Prague Airport, had hailed a bakery van and ridden into town with a load of fragrant loaves. It was going to work out, because these two train attendants were still with us and, above all, Marlou and I were still with each other. And now there was a third, just as Marlou is one, I am another, and our relationship adds up to three. And the third here and now took the form of the chief of station operations for Aix-en-Provence. He had on a blue cap, wore a blue jacket and was all business. This is how the French held on to Morocco. He wasn't going to let us go.

Which explains why, less than half an hour later, my electric wheelchair had been loaded into the back of a rented Renault van, and Marlou and I were driving toward our hotel. Marlou was worried about getting lost, and I kept telling her that she was a miraculous person. As was I. Before me was one map, thirty roads and fifty choices. I chose the right one because it didn't matter. The signs kept coming at me, confusing and inconsistent. I am not used to driving on the Continent. It didn't matter. All the signs were pointing the right way.

Skin

NOVEMBER 2007

I am leaving France under a cloud, under a gun, and under a shower.

I have been trying to extract some deeper meaning from the latter. But the more I try, the more I feel like some ancient practitioner of necromancy, poking around the entrails instead of just giving up and letting them be, well, entrails.

In fact, the more I think about it, the entire scene is pure Samuel Beckett. I have rolled my wheelchair up to the edge of the Novotel shower. This shower and, in fact, this hotel have been chosen for this very purpose. Modernity, wheelchair access, safety. So, it's easy to drop my legs over the edge of the bathtub, carefully position both – one leg moving under its own neurological steam, the other shoved into place like a department store mannequin – then grab the one handrail opposite. By sliding my butt to the very edge of the wheelchair, leaning forward and grabbing the handrail, I can stand. I am now vertical, in the bathtub with its hand-held shower head on a stainless steel cable, my soap on its accustomed rope on my hand. All quadriplegic systems are go for wash. Turn on the water.

The showerhead is, being hand-held, currently sitting very low on its convenient perch. The spray is pointing sideways, toward the front of the bathtub, the gentle water washing along the tiles, down the wall, and over my feet. What happens, in the way of such things, is that the gentle turns. It turns hot. It turns that way, because I have just twisted the faucet control slightly to the left. The water has leapt from tepid to scalding. My limbs are leaping too. They are leaping because they are neurologically out-of-control. I have only one small handrail to hold onto. I have to make an immediate decision. Let go and try to control the temperature, i.e., turn the water off – and in so doing, possibly fall. Everything is leaping and jumping, my limbs are trying desperately to flail and toss and knock me off balance. It's a long way down, and at the bottom it's all porcelain. My arm is burning, my foot is burning. I am holding on for dear life. I cannot control this. I have to end it. I scream for help. I scream again, "Help."

Marlou is there in seconds. "Turn it off," I say. Unfortunately, my body is in the way, and so is my wheelchair, and Marlou has to maneuver around both to get to the water. It's off now. And so, it seems, is much of my skin.

My left arm has achieved a deep lobster color. And my foot? It feels that something is terribly amiss, but no, Marlou takes a look at it, and so do I. The foot seems okay. The arm? Not so okay. About as not okay as a bad sunburn. Which isn't reassuring, actually, because all these events have occurred in the neurological haze of quadriplegia. I can't really feel what's going on in my skin, yet I have to live in it. My skin, that is. What to do? Well, nothing much for the time being. Marlou and I have some sightseeing to do, after all, and I try to calm her worries, sooth my doubts, and get us both out the door. To one of the glorious hill districts of Provence.

After all, Marlou is equipped with a certain amount of first-aid gear. And after a spray of this, and a bandaging of that, we are underway. In fact, in the *pharmacie de l'ocre* we buy additional bandages. The pharmacist offers the traditional French advice. That is to say, I roll up my sleeve and show the woman the reddened skin. She doesn't flinch, but suggests this bandage and that one. We have had an authentic French experience, have purchased some EU approved first-aid antiseptic and are on our way.

We had what, for Provence, passes as a modest lunch. Instead of the pull-out-all-the-stops *gastronomie* of the previous day, I settle for some roasted Provençal peppers and a lasagna. Still, I feel that I have eaten what I normally ingest in approximately three days in California. Never mind, for this repast has been more or less light by my travel standards. We load the wheelchair back in the van – that is to say, Marlou does – and I marvel at how all this wheelchair schlepping has worked out.

Down the autoroute, back to the hotel, and Marlou makes my electric wheelchair walk the plank for the absolute last time. Later, I try to have something light in the hotel dining room. The menu sports a page of healthy alternatives, with an introductory paragraph extolling the virtues of grilling on a plank. It's a wrought iron plank, and if you believe the copy, "almost no oil is required" to prepare your very healthy meal. I order the shrimp with mixed vegetables. What can I say? There's plenty of Provençal olive oil, some deep-fried vegetables, and some sort of artisan sauce that may be the archetypal precursor to tartar sauce.

It's gone in an instant, and I would be too, except that it's 10:30 p.m. and my cousin Bob has just blown in from Paris, via the TGV. We have a delightful drink, the three of us. It gets late. I go back to my room, slip off my shoe and stare in horror at the enormous white blister that has risen along the side of my foot. We call Bob in his room. We three stare at my foot. No one likes the look of my arm, either. I am half resigned to seeing a doctor the next day. It will make Marlou feel better, and the next morning Bob says it will make him feel better, too. Being a worrier, a little medical attention will also make me feel better.

Instead, we take the easier course. The following morning, we have the usual spectacular assortment of bakery goods, accompanied by coffee, and followed by, yes, another visit to a pharmacie. Actually, this marks our third. Bob has been out early that morning and purchased a healing balm. Now we need more bandages, I produce my arm one more time, and both Bob and Marlou cluck approval. The redness has gone down. Less lobster, more rapidly improving sunburn. As for the blister, we now have an entirely second opinion from the second pharmacist of the day: leave it alone.

After some screwing about, we hit the road again, wheelchair loaded, Bob somehow loaded into his own seat in the back (thus the miracle of our Renault Kangoo) – and we now have a lunch that does considerable damage to what is left of my body. Provençal beef stew. And followed by one of the most imaginative, and utterly decadent, chocolate desserts on record: a sort of chocolate satire on Vietnamese spring rolls. They even have a dipping sauce (ginger).

Thus the gun, and the cloud, and the shower. We've been traveling for almost a month now. My body has had it. The shower thing? Just a reminder. I don't live here. I live there.

Gypsies

NOVEMBER 2007

The farmer in the home across the road from my cousin Caroline knows all about his neighbor, the Jewish doctor. If Caroline is something of a character in these parts, so is the farmer, John. There's a tractor and all sorts of impressive farm machinery behind his house, and I assume the fields beyond must belong to him. But what I really know about John is his barbecue. He hauls an enormous grill behind his tractor in the warmer months, going from one party to the next. John, barbecue man. I found him leaning against a fence with his son. Actually, we found him. It was Marlou who said hello.

Why does this detail matter? Because in California, of the two of us, Marlou is less likely to approach a total stranger and initiate chitchat. But we are traveling, after all, and all bets are off, all roles are reversed and nothing is what it usually seems. Which explains why Marlou remembered John's name, though I didn't, and the two of us approached, me in my wheelchair, to join him by his side fence. John does not actually chew on a piece of grass, but this is probably only under advice of his dentist. One has to imagine the grass. His Gloucestershire accent makes him almost incomprehensible. So, conversation naturally drifted to the big regional news of the year: cousin Caroline's near-death experience in the Gloucestershire floods.

"The doctor tried to park her car in a river." That was how John put it.

"The doctor doesn't take advice." That's how I put it.

"We know that," said John.

With that, Marlou and I were away. There was something astonishing up the road, an apparition I had glimpsed from the first-floor window of the bedroom that serves as my office in Caroline and Alistair's Todenham home. A Gypsy wagon, painted, carved, and drawn by two draft horses, which looked like miniature Clydesdales, had just clip-clopped down the road. Marlou, having seen the same thing, had rushed out to get a better look. And sure enough, just over a rise, there they were. One Gypsy wagon. Two horses. Three generations of Romany. Plus conventional vehicles, including two old cars and one battered aluminum caravan. As we approached, Marlou warned me. You don't have to make a point. This is who these people are, just enjoy them and get out. Marlou is recalling that I'm not always generous with Seventh-Day Adventists, Mormons and the other religiously demented who occasionally knock on our apartment door.

Sure enough, within minutes the old woman standing beside the circus-wagon-looking hunk of wooden rolling stock had gone rolling off in the direction of fundamentalist Christianity. What a beautiful wagon, I said. Oh yes, she said, we have this beauty in honor of Jesus. Have you found Jesus? Oh, yes, I said, vaguely nodding and remembering to get a good look at the view of Gloucestershire beyond. It was, after all, a remarkably sunny and crisp October day, not the sort of thing one takes for granted in autumnal England. Jesus has saved me, the woman said. The horses are beautiful, I said, convinced that there was no opener here for Jesus, Christianity or general salvation. What kind are they, I asked? The woman stared at them blankly. They're called piebald, she said. Even I knew this referred to coloring, not to breed, but I let this pass. Before she could get in another word about Jesus, I said something about the impressive size of the horses' hooves. The latter were enormously wide, very shaggy with hair above the shins or forelegs or whatever the horse-savvy call them. Oh, yes, she said. When had I found Jesus?

The breeze blew, Gloucestershire wavered, green and glorious, at the bottom of the hill where a horse-drawn railway once headed to the neighboring village of Shipston. I know just enough of the local lore to appreciate, and increasingly love, this spot. Which was why even an evangelical gypsy could not throw me off my conversational stride. Found Jesus? Didn't know he was lost. I said none of this. Just smiled. Beautiful wagon, I added. Did you make it yourself? Oh, no, she said. You need a special tool to do that sort of thing. What sort of thing? Oh the carving and that, she said. You could paint the red bits yourself, but that's real gold there on those other bits. You need a special tool. Where are you from, she asked? California, I said. Oh, that's in American, isn't it? Oh I've never flown in an airplane, but I will now, if I have to, since I've found Jesus. As this rolled by me, rote and mechanical, I wondered how Jesus had found the Romany. These people used to be known for picking pockets in the village marketplace. Now they had gone straight, apparently, and were busily picking up converts. I didn't get it. I didn't want to. I'd seen the cart and the horses and the view, and that would do. I had a final go at conversation. Where was she born? Worcestershire. I frowned and looked as puzzled as I could. Worcestershire? Where is that on the map, I asked? England, she said. Ah. I clicked my wheelchair into gear and bounced back along the road.

Solar Plexus

FEBRUARY 2007

The solar plexus begins draining somewhere over Iceland. Not that you are necessarily over Iceland. For, in fact, all you really know is that it's night, the cabin lights are off and all wise passengers are asleep. Most went to sleep after dinner, which was only about 7:30 p.m. California time, but the more sensible travelers are already on London time, eight hours ahead. But why be sensible? I haven't made this trip in awhile, and I'm excited.

A chance to connect with Britain and things British, to be with extended family. To be with my extended self, which feels at home in the UK and always imagines returning.

The thing about the solar plexus is that one doesn't really know how much it can drain. I mean, how much stuff is in there? And what is the "stuff"? It feels very much like the stuff of life, and the later one stays up, and the more one sits in an airline seat, breathing airline air and interacting with airline employees, the more sickening the whole experience feels. Why would anyone name an airline "Virgin"? Nothing about this experience seems virginal, let alone pure. The cabin crew have been around the service sector block, one can tell. They are smiling and helpful to the point of excess. Not that I mind, exactly. My real objection has to do with the buxom, red-cheeked and very English young woman who keeps calling me "honey," which just doesn't work coming out of an English mouth. This is an American expression, one that I associate with my wife or a waitress in a coffee shop in the Deep South. Actually, I know why I am being honeyed. I am old. I do wear my trousers rolled, and now I am so safely nonthreatening as to be a British flight attendant's honey.

But soon I'm too tired to worry about this. I have other fish to fry. Intestinal fish, for example. I keep thinking about the distance between my seat and the toilet. I regret drinking all that iodine for my pre-trip CT scan. Either I have a hernia or I don't. There's not much I can do about it over Iceland. But it is over Iceland that I finally work out the obvious. The same iodine mothers used to dab over cuts, producing a nicely antiseptic blood-like stain on the skin, probably does the same thing to the intestinal tract. I cinch my seatbelt a bit tighter, then loosen it. Everything under the seatbelt is loosened already – that's the problem. And I now understand that this intestinal loosening is due to iodine. Which isn't meant to be dumped into one's digestive system any more than one is meant to fly. No wonder something in me is losing the will to go on as this trip approaches 1 a.m., California time. I can't read anymore. I can't watch another film. And yet when the lights suddenly come on and I lift the window shade to stare at morning over the Outer Hebrides, my spirits lift too. Who knows if those are really the Hebrides. All one can see is clouds, which do get more impressive as we turn over the Irish Sea, this latter detail verified by the captain. Big, white cumulus clouds, powerful and playful at the same time. And dammit if I'm not feeling playful myself. I am more than half paralyzed, sixty years old, and I need all the play I can get.

The wheelchair pushers employed by the British Airports Authority give the impression of having acquired a good education and a solid knowledge of the world. The man who pushes me through Heathrow seems to get older as we cross an English county or two, such are the distances. There's something happening here, something in the sum total of Czech Airways, Gulf Air and Air Dubai. Why does one need an enormous 747 to fly to a dinky principality on the Persian Gulf? There's something happening here, and it has to do with the modern world, and at sixty years of age, it's too much for me. The Heathrow man fills in my landing card, for which I am infinitely grateful. The immigration woman asks me whom I am visiting. For a moment, I can't recall. Am I visiting? Or do I live here? Never mind, she implies, stamping my passport.

I am pushed into the enormous customs hall, and I'm relieved to find that my real wheelchair, the one with batteries, is fully functional and rolling toward me, with its night lights on. I overlook this detail, hauling myself up from the plastic airport wheelchair and into the real manly thing. We set off, the Heathrow man and I, for the train. I flash my out-of-date British rail card hoping for the disabled discount, and the clerk doesn't bat an eye, producing a bargain round-trip ticket. Not that anything in Britain is a bargain for Americans these days. I don't understand what's happened to our dollar, but then I don't really understand what's happened to our nation. And never mind all that, for the time being. For I'm on a train, and if I wasn't on this one I would be on the next one. Which would have manifested in fifteen minutes. And in fact, fifteen minutes is all it takes to whoosh from Heathrow to Paddington Station at the edge of the

West End. The world is supposed to be like this. And the world gets even better at Paddington, where an affable Nigerian drives up in a golf cart with a blue wheelchair symbol on it, flings my bags in the back and drives me to the handicapped waiting room. Yes, these days there is one. There, the man stacks my luggage in a corner and tells me to keep an eye on the bags. Yes, this is Britain too, the land of petty theft. I'm feeling petty myself, and suddenly have an insurmountable need to read the morning's *Guardian*. I want to know who Gordon Brown really is. I want to know how deeply *Guardian* journalists feel the shame of the UK being ranked second in the United Nations' report on countries with bad conditions for young people. The United States is first in this list, and I cringe at the knowledge that some in my country take this as a sort of compliment.

In any event, this is what the *Guardian* promises, and it's what I need. I roll out of the handicapped waiting room and find myself in a jostling sea of people. In Britain, railway stations are still alive. People actually use them, people in huge numbers. No, I don't want an *Evening Standard*, the newspaper currently on sale in the newsagents' stalls around the platforms. Though I regularly bought the afternoon edition when I was headed home on the Tube, thirty-five years ago. And is it possible that I actually walked everywhere, even trudging through cavernous Paddington Station with a crutch? I doubt that anyone here would believe me today. I barely believe this historical fact myself.

For now, I roll inside WH Smith, give a Bengali seventy pence and roll out. Back to the handicapped waiting room before my bags are stolen. Which, of course, is unlikely for there is an actual staff of people in this office carrying elderly persons to and from trains, accompanying wheelchair users like me, and generally keeping the lame, halt and blind on the move around southern Britain. When it's time for my train, I've made it enough into the *Guardian* to know I've made it in general. The Great Western train blasts toward Oxford and beyond. It actually achieves train speeds in the ninety-mph range, although it has to stop frequently for passengers who want to step off at the likes of Kingham and drive through all these beautiful green fields, fresh, breezy and full of standing water. The conductor asks me where I'm going, and I tell her "God only knows." She laughs. Britain.

Moreton-in-Marsh, my station, and my batteries are charged, and my solar plexus is once again whole.

Love for Three Hundred Oranges

FEBRUARY 2007

These days, it's my cousin's sixtieth birthday too, more exactly my cousins', Caroline and Bob, and the event is assuming epic proportions. The Cotswolds Marquee Company has called round with their heated tent, and the thing is now up and ready for action. God only knows where the heat comes from – Alastair, Caroline's husband says that something burns, perhaps kerosene or paraffin, and the heater heats... it's that simple. God also only knows where the people are coming from, all one-hundred-fifty of them. That's why what is already a large country home now has a plastic annex, the polythene walls flapping in the late-winter wind. By my guess, at least one-third of the Gloucestershire village of Todenham is turning up for this affair. This notion makes me vaguely uncomfortable, but not to worry. That's why God invented introverts. And although I fear the social demands of one hundred villagers, virtually none of whom I know, and the few of whom I know having names I don't remember... the whole remarkable thing intrigues me. It's a party, a big one. Now We Are Sixty.

The kitchen is chaos. Who would guess that this authentically English eighteenth-century farm home is full of Jews arguing about food? The menu includes a couscous chicken dish, but the recipe is in dispute. In fact everything is in dispute. Not only do no two people agree on how to prepare the meal, there is also wide disagreement on how to preserve it.

Chopping, dicing, mincing, stirring, not to mention peeling

and husking, have begun days before the party. At the center of current controversy: what to do about the oranges. Several hundred have been peeled and sliced, and are now being stored in a plastic garbage can. By "stored," one means placed outside. The temperature approaches 0 degrees Celsius, so the outside is the refrigerator. This works splendidly at night, but most of us have little faith in the daytime. The temperature approached that of a cold California day this afternoon, and the oranges were on everyone's minds. Caroline insisted they could be left alone, that no harm would come to them in the final twenty-four hours pre-launch. I was of the opposite opinion, that given another mild afternoon like this one, we would have a sort of crude version of Cointreau ripening in the garbage can. Jake, Caroline's son, had a much more retail-display approach to the problem. Cut up some fresh oranges at the last minute, he suggested, place them on top, and no one will know the difference. Anyone digging down to the lower layer of old, mashed, and bacteriologically compromised oranges will probably be too drunk to know the difference.

Kitchen work is a great leveler. So is time. During my four years in Britain, almost forty years ago, I watched as my second cousins advanced in careers, developed relationships, got their lives together, it seemed. In my competitive and envious sense of things, I was falling behind. I cut myself little slack, as they say, barely acknowledging that falling behind was probably better than falling over. Which I rarely did. I don't recall falling over on my daily quarter-mile walk to the local tube station, stumbling as I boarded buses or tripping over the heavy old carpets in my bedsitting room. Every disabled day was difficult, from showering to shopping. And the falling behind part haunted me constantly. Would I ever have a job, a girlfriend, a life?

These days, sitting in Caroline's Cotswold kitchen, observing others at work, some of these old feelings return. I do feel useless. Something in me emotionally tightens up when it's time to speak, to take the floor and demand attention. I don't know what I'm saying. I'm not British. I'm not good enough to be here and be part of things. Caroline and Bob have real jobs and real accomplishments. My only accomplishment is that I have survived. Survived to not only fight another day, but to have another day, and make it here for this day. To make it six thousand miles. To make it out the door and through the rain puddles of Todenham. Crocuses are bursting through the grass by the Todenham town hall. How do I know they were crocuses? A passing villager told me. I've had enough isolation and loneliness in my life to appreciate a casual chat with a passing stranger. A passing acquaintance. A passing moment, and one captured on my second cousin's mobile phone camera.

This is really what's made the difference, at least half of it. There's another generation now. Jake and Alexandra readily ridicule me, bring me cups of tea and treat me like an immutable member of the family. Something in me is more or less their age emotionally, so I feel quite comfortable with their badinage. Some things have been healed within me, while others have healed with time's passage in the world around me. It may look like the depth of winter to a Californian, but the crocuses are coming up. It's warmer – all of it – than I think.

The Amniotic Coast

DECEMBER 2005

"She's never visited us," my mother-in-law observes. "But, then, she's always looking for meaning. And there's not much meaning over here."

She is speaking of a friend, the only friend who has never appeared on her doorstep, her current doorstep for the last twenty-five years, her Hawaiian doorstep. Everyone else, it seems, has turned up since the in-laws moved here from Los Angeles in 1980. Marlou and I are visiting for Christmas, and this talk of the absence of meaning round about Hawaii is making me nervous. No, "nervous" isn't very apt, and "anxious" doesn't capture it either. Actually, I am no worse than mildly unsettled. It's hard to get more than mildly anything in the Hawaiian Islands. Very hard.

It is the final day of our visit, Christmas Day, to be precise. Chestnuts may be roasting on an open fire somewhere, but we are having drinks and looking at the tropical bay. The water is dappled with various shades of turquoise and sky blue, remarkably transparent even this close to Honolulu. Low tide reveals arcing coral. The reefs here are said to be making an environmental comeback. I am making a comeback too, having spent a week and a half on these shores. I am wavering and wafting as gently as the distant waves. I am seeing things without focusing on them. It is unclear whether I am seeing but not focusing, focusing not seeing, or neither, or both. What is very clear is that I don't give a flying fuck. The last time I drank this early in the afternoon was, well, yesterday. And probably the day before. Although I'm not really clear on the day before. Not to say that I couldn't nail down the facts if the local district attorney insisted. But he isn't, is he? Insisting, I mean.

No, it isn't drink. It's Hawaii. And just in case you have a spinal cord injury, do not perspire normally and cannot regulate your body heat, don't assume that my condition has something to do with excessive air temperature or humidity. It has to do with what we did Christmas Eve. We went for a drive. Not even a particularly spectacular drive, but a fairly short jaunt up the coast to a bird refuge. On the way back, birds identified and everyone satisfied, we rounded a bay, a completely ordinary inlet with semicircular symmetry, waters of transparent blue lapping against a narrow white strip of beach, coconut palms draped over the sand like compliant street lamps. Just one of your ordinary Polynesian scenes. Tropical fruits within easy reach. Tropical maidens not much further. This sort of scene that completes itself instantly, presenting a tropical alternative to everything else. And if you're Paul Gauguin, and that everything-else amounts to the rest of your life in a poorly ventilated Paris bank, or if you're Fletcher Christian, and one option is white sand and brown breasts and the other is wooden bunks and Captain Bly, well, it's kind of a no-brainer, isn't it?

Everything in Hawaii is a no-brainer, because the brain is not in control. The cortex has been demoted, downgraded, and generally dismissed for lack of performance. Pores are in the driver's seat. The hair is alert. Certain parts of the neuro-anatomy perform a passive, intelligence-gathering function, but that's about it. Most of the body has been given over to lulling and lolling. In Hawaii one floats. Progress is measured in getting out, if you are able-bodied, standing up, if you're crippled. Polynesian paralysis, locals call it. Whatever it's called, there's no escaping it. Even in an air-conditioned car, curving the highway length of a lagoon, it will seize you. And yes, you Mr. Smarty-Pants with your long list of must-read literary works, you will find yourself deep into a murder mystery. Every word of which seems unaccountably vivid and profound. That is to say, having found meaning in the likes of Elmore Leonard, you are now ready to begin a doctorate thesis on the cross-fertilization of weltschmerz in Yanni and Karen Carpenter. And when you snap to and realize that for the last four hours you have been so deeply engrossed in waves and midriffs that you cannot remember the difference between a Mai Tai and a water ski, well, that's the time to turn the page. If you have the strength.

Under such circumstances, you can understand why Hawaiians leave much to geology. When your island is framed by idyllic coastline, lots of other things more or less take care of themselves. Which is why the best of Hawaii is pleasantly funky. Take lunch. On the day of the bird outing, the in-laws guided us directly to an authentic Southern barbecue in an authentic semi-abandoned Hawaiian strip mall. Which, on closer examination, proved to be an entirely inaccurate impression. First, every commercial inch of the cinderblock edifice was occupied. It included a post office, which happened to be closed for lunch. Never mind that lunch had extended well past 2 p.m., for if you had to choose between correlating zip codes with carrier routes versus, say, gauging wave heights and cleavage depths, you might just post the "back at" sign yourself. As for the barbecue, like many a booming Hawaiian business, it had a way of concealing itself. Like having no permanent sign, just a plastic banner with a Pepsi logo proclaiming "Uncle Bobo's Barbecue," with one end of the fabric unsecured and folded, concealing just enough letters to make you wonder if this was a barbecue or a bar. No doubt about the food. True smoky barbecue, rich and satisfying. The place is thriving.

As was I. On the day of our departure, the 8 a.m. sun in the low seventies and a pleasant breeze enlivening the bedroom, I found it very difficult to put on my pants. Not that I had worn any for the last ten days. Perhaps I was really finding it difficult to accept the idea of pants. Having a sort of Platonic crisis. What are pants for? Are they an image or a thing? Or, was my body sliding perilously close to the end of the speed control dial? Shifting from slow to stop? Or perhaps it was trying to explore the meaning of "stop." But probably not. Meaning, as every true Hawaiian knows, is for the mainland.

Cherubs of the Amniotic Coast

JANUARY 2006

I'm not sure why it's called Princeville, nor does the question even occur to me while I'm sitting on the terrace of the Princeville Resort enjoying a stunning omelet. The omelet is vying with the view for my attention and wins by a slight margin, for it will soon turn cold and the view will not. Such is my reasoning. It is all the reasoning I can manage at this moment on the Amniotic Coast. We will face the next moment if and when we come to it.

Whatever the origins of the Princeville Resort, sitting on its terrace having breakfast makes me feel like a prince. For wasn't this a princely idea, getting up early and driving to the northern end of Kauai to take one's morning meal in inexpensive luxury? The omelet proves to be so rich and savory, sporting both bacon and avocado, that I'm forced to take my gastrointestinal time. Between forkfuls, I gaze down from the cliffside hotel at the sweeping bay, where waves obediently mass half a mile from shore, gently lifting surfers as they crest. The waves roll in at an endless diagonal, showing off the curve of the coast, the white of the distant sand, the volcanic black of the sheer Polynesian mountains. The magnificence of the scene is truly cinematic, and this is not a turn of phrase but a fact of film history. "South Pacific" was filmed on the beach below me.

So why is it that from the warm and liquid depths of the day, in this moment of high pampering and indulgence, of tropical scenery and cholesterol, I am beginning to feel uncomfortable about the Princeville Resort? Maybe the decor. Someone not terribly in tune with things Polynesian has fancied up the place. The restaurant furniture, tubular-steel Louis XVI, doesn't fit. The lobby's crystal chandeliers are so outsparkled by the glinting Pacific as to seem silly. As for the Italianate statuary, one plaster cherub hangs off the terrace railing just to my right, slightly obscuring my view of the promontory used as South Pacific's "Bali Hai." But, okay, so the hotel decorators didn't get it, so what? The decor is there to raise the tone, or at least the room rates. Because in the real world, Polynesian splendor probably isn't worth four hundred dollars a night without a touch of Caesar's Palace. The real world as defined by business, that is. Which defines everything these days, particularly in America. Where the real world has never been more unreal.

It was too much to expect human beings to receive the gift of Hawaii as a gift. Even as the Polynesians waded ashore from their Thor Heyerdahl rafts around 1000 A.D., the first of humankind's environmental depredations sauntered in behind them. The pigs, real ones with curlicue tales, occupied the rafts, and soon the barbecue pits. Of course, within minutes the pigs were bounding through the Hawaiian jungles, digging up roots and munching bird eggs. These remote islands were so protected by thousands of miles of open ocean that even mosquitoes hadn't arrived. Until something, probably bilge water expelled from an anchoring ship, introduced mosquitoes to the Hawaiian Islands in the early 1800s. With disastrous results for species unused to having their blood sucked and sullied. In such an idyllic, utterly isolated land, where magnificent birds nest on the ground like sitting ducks, literally and metaphorically, it didn't take much to start losing whole species. Today, on top of feral pigs, the islands have feral cats, and feral chickens, along with the occasional mongoose and rat. Altogether people have despoiled Hawaii. Not because they meant to, but because they usually can't help it.

On the other hand, there are the taro fields. Marlou wandered about them just a couple of days before. No one can tell me exactly what taro is, or why the Hawaiians cultivate it so enthusiastically, but there it is, growing in flooded fields, much like rice. I've seen rice farmed in equally boggy acreage north of Sacramento. The difference is that in parched California, flooding fields raises eyebrows, particularly when you're pouring tax-supported water over your crop. In rainy Hawaii no one worries about the water, but developers certainly eye the land, and setting aside hotel-ready property to raise taro root raises an entirely different set of eyebrows. The miracle is that in both places, California and Hawaii, human restraint has prevailed and nature has, in a small way, prevailed too. In California's arid central valley, flooded fields may attract attention, but they also attract birds. The rice fields double as bird sanctuary. Hawaii's taro fields do the same, and Hawaiian fish and game people keep an eye on the preserve.

Sharing with the animals, pulling back, making room. This isn't our natural tendency. But it's close to our highest achievement. It represents lessons learned, or taught, in humanity's oldest myths. That God or nature or whatever one wants to call that which is so much greater than ourselves and allows us to live and die and drink coffee and watch HBO, that force is worthy of respect. If not worship. America's most vocally religious decry the rise of things secular, but they seem to overlook things imperial. What could be more imperious than trying to upstage a volcano with a plaster cherub? Especially if you believe that the cherub will outlast the volcano. Trust me, it won't.

Windward

DECEMBER 2008

Why do disabled people love to travel? They do, you know. The web is full of advice for wheelchair travelers. And the most obvious recommendation is nowhere to be seen: stay home.

At home you are less likely to slide out of control down a cobblestone street, get stuck at the top of a thousand marble steps or break your wheelchair axle a continent away from the nearest dealer. So, why do we travel? I was wondering this while at an airport waiting for a bus. There should have been no wait at all. The driver of the number 20 bus assured me that I should catch the number 19 bus behind him. And the number 19, its operator said, was very much the wrong one, and did the number 20 guy really tell me to wait for him? With that, both buses departed. And I had a good half an hour to consider the general merits of, and rationale for, disabled travel.

It was a good half an hour, because I went to all the bad places. These include blaming myself for whatever goes wrong in my life. And going to the bad place is the good thing about travel. The bad places are always the most instructive. And they do have a way of bracing the spirit and inspiring action. I resolved that the next bus, whatever its number, would be my bus. I would take it. The driver could say whatever he wished, but I was boarding. And so it came to pass that the number 20 stopped, the wheelchair lift extended, and I rose like a deus ex machina into the maw of the Waikiki Downtown Express. The bus's interior was deeply air-conditioned, the refrigeration bringing into stark contrast the abundant tropical warmth, airport kerosene and diesel fumes notwithstanding.

The driver refused my fare. The same happens to me in San Francisco and in the suburbs to the south, now here in Hawaii, so this must be part of the universal disabled experience. What does it mean? That being disabled automatically inspires sympathy? That most disabled people are financially strapped? Who can say? I can say one thing. My vibes on boarding the number twenty Waikiki are not the strongest. I am very aware of the precariousness of my disabled state. My journey depends entirely on the mechanical fortitude of a wheelchair, the only lifeline to the outside world my mobile phone. Yet, as the number twenty rumbles along a street named Nimitz, the adventure of disabled travel begins to manifest. Who in Honolulu takes a bus? This old guy and his apparent wife, he with a U.S. Army cap and she with a sour expression. This middle-aged woman, loose and fleshy in her capacious muumuu, carrying a shopping bag. A family, forty-five-ish guy with twenty-something kids, all somehow the same age. Until the bus's recorded announcement tells us that this is King Street and Aleimena, transfer point for the windward buses.

Traveling, being down on the ground, where the difference between catching and missing a bus is tangible, one pricks up the ears at "windward." This is how Hawaiians express geography. There is, apparently, wind on one side of the islands, less on the other, and it pays to know the difference if you want to get anywhere. Just as it pays to listen to a London cab driver when he tells you not to request the east side of Queens Park –"don't give me any compass, mate" – but to say it's near the Duke of York, the neighborhood pub.

So, now I'm in central Honolulu, looking up at a high-rise bank, and waiting with other hapless souls for the number 55 Windward. I perch my throbbing, swelling, paralyzed leg on a marble ledge, and twice within a few minutes someone from the bank comes outside to sponge the rainwater off the bench. The first person appears to be a sort of bank porter, and the second is a bona fide janitor. Both smile at me. This is what they do, post-rain marble drying. Both are doubtless from the Philippines. Thus, Hawaii. I am in what could be called a nice part of town. This, I theorize, underlies the difference of opinion between bus drivers. This route, the longer one, involves a change of buses here. The other, who knows?

At last the number 55 rolls up and we roll away. I am relieved, feeling more confident now about man and his future. My wife is slowly dying. We both say this now. And my confidence in everything is, well, different. More than ever, I am learning to take things as they come. And they're coming at me right now, as the number 55 climbs a small hill and heads away from the center of Honolulu. A native Hawaiian, about my age, has befriended a thirty-ish guy beside him. The younger man explains that he is a schoolteacher, here in Hawaii to interview for a job in an intermediate school. And on his modest income, he appreciates this two-dollar transit ride along the northern edge of the island of Oahu. I appreciate it too. The older one, the Hawaiian native, can't stop talking. There is this bus and that bus and the other, and the schoolteacher would be wise to take them all. What's that? The schoolteacher is asking about a sign to the Punch Bowl something or other. This, I know, is a famous military cemetery.

The older Hawaiian knows it too and expresses himself this way: "Oh, that's where the service guys who have been in the military they give them the graves so the soldiers can be buried there with the veterans when they die." There is something authentically Hawaiian in this circumlocution, and I find it pleasing. The bus accelerates, slipping into the fast road over the Pali, the volcanic ridge where Hawaiian kings famously threw human sacrifices over the edge. I doze ever so briefly, perhaps absorbing the knowledge that my ride aboard the number 55 will stretch to approximately two hours.

We descend into Kaneohe, which might be called a suburb of Honolulu, but really shouldn't be. The island is too small for that sort of thing. Kaneohe is its own separate town. My in-laws live here, and my wife and I will visit here shortly, so the look of the place is not unfamiliar. The volcanic mountains in the background make it a spectacular place. The complete absence of hotels makes this a remarkably un-touristy part of a tourist island. Puddles gleam everywhere, and the grass at the edge of the road ripples like a green meadow. This place has had a lot of rain. At one bus stop, ten high school kids climb aboard. At the next, a black woman, perhaps late thirties, and a hobbling white guy about ten years older. One or both reek of alcohol. The woman carries a passel of bags. One, a plastic shopping bag, is full of aluminum cans, empty and half crushed. The look on her face, also empty and half crushed, lies beyond sadness. She sits at the end of a bench closest to me. Instinctively, I pull back, look away. Perhaps she will talk to me, demand my attention, ask me for money. Even if she asks only for pity, my coffers are empty.

We pass the main Kaneohe shopping mall, with Sears and Starbucks and Barnes & Noble. People get on, people get off. And just at the edge of town, before the highway slips into an authentic mangrove swamp, the black woman and her limping companion get off with all their bags. I often forget that I live in the soft world and that most of the world is hard. The road now leads somewhere between the two. We are now a country bus, passing the Hygienic Store, its name probably dating from the era of sugar plantations. Further on, the highway arcs along a true tropical lagoon, palm trees in a circle along a bay. Bali Hai. Waves lap at the road. The houses set along it are built on stilts, raised high above the frequent floods. At the local branch of Brigham Young University, a beautiful young woman gets off. At the next stop, an aging beach bum slips from bus to forest.

The quadriplegic species does not survive because it is the fittest. In Darwinian terms, I should have succumbed long ago. I survive because I have, in the splendid words of Tennessee Williams, always relied on the kindness of strangers. What else can one call it but kindness or generosity or, yes, charity? My existence is fragile, and I can feel this more immediately bouncing west on the number 55. Here is one of the lessons of travel, the interdependence of human beings. In the United States, where self-reliance, self-starting, self-everything, is so highly prized, the lesson of disabled travel always comes down to this: we are all on a journey. So don't sneer at the black woman with the recycled cans, the beach bum who is too old to be bumming. We all owe each other something. What it is, and how and when we repay, life will tell us.

Now we are passing the shrimp farms. These are unprepossessing ponds, murky and muddy, each square and lined with reeds. Their harvest is for sale from the vans and shacks along the highway. Island's best shrimp. Legendary shrimp van. Hottest shrimp. Much of what's on offer in Hawaii is like this. Splintering and funky and expressed in pidgin native dialect. Shave ice. Store is close. In between the big hotels are many miles of small towns and small shops. Country. As a traveler, I can only pass through it, never know it. There is a culture and a way of life here, and it is immune to assaults by travelers. When we stop at a high school, pass a particular row of shops, speed by the shrimp vans, our bus driver launches into a flurry of commentary. I can tell by his general intonation that he is uttering slogans, satirical or sincerely emblematic, one cannot say. I do not understand more than ten percent of what he says.

Flowers, hibiscus or something like them, sprout from a carefully tended hedge woven through a fence. A golf course lies beyond. And now the bus turns from the highway, down a private road passing, of all things, a guard station. This is a gated community of sorts. It is my hotel. The bus stops, the wheelchair lift drops me to the ground, and I weave through a waiting knot of hotel maids and golf course attendants to the distant lobby. There, I do not roll through a door, because there is no door. There is not even a front wall. This is Hawaii. Land of the wall-less. My door is always open, because it isn't. And there in the lobby is my wife calling to me.

I tried to call her about half an hour before, as the bus was rounding its lagoon. But I had forgotten her number. Such a thing is not possible. I know my wife's mobile phone number. But such things are happening these days. These days may be our last. And what does this mean? How many are there? Haven't I had abundant opportunity to make some distracted move between Honolulu Airport and here that would end my own life? Is it the fact of death we fear or the separation from the one we love? What happens when there is no mobile phone and no number and no answer?

Marlou's parents have driven her from the airport, my two-hundred-pound electric wheelchair being far too bulky for any normal car or van. Disabled travel is built around such realities. The Honolulu taxi company has a wheelchair-lift-equipped van that last year drove me here for $175. The money seems a waste. I got here today for one dollar. Marlou's parents joke about the bus ride. Over lunch, someone in the golf course restaurant has heard about my transit plight and offers condolences. I assure that person none are necessary.

Marlou's parents seem friendly but distracted. They leave quickly. Marlou tells me about her talk with them, all about her and cancer and time left. They all needed some privacy. I needed a journey.

The Bridge

DECEMBER 2010

Winter light. The low slanting sun pries up thoughts, loosens memories. Which is why it is a good idea to sit outside at Café Borrone, even in December, or especially in December, cold be damned. Actually, with my back to the sun, the California morning's solar heating is enough to get me through an entire latte, sufficiently caffeinated to face anything. And what I'm facing for once is pleasantly mild. Something my friend Bruce, who reigns along with me on the Caltrain Advisory Committee, said regarding Eurostar, the London-Paris high-speed train. He had heard from a friend that the trip was not very interesting. No, no, no, I assured him.

Perhaps Bruce's friend had meant that the sub-Channel train ride was not particularly scenic. Not that it matters, though I would disagree even on that score. The experience is as unscenic as being launched into low earth orbit. The view may be confined to a tiny porthole and a bunch of dials, but there's a lot going on. And you know it. That is the thing.

First, there is the launch pad, London's refurbished, restored, and forgive me, re-visioned St. Pancras Station. An utterly mad Victorian folly of bricks and chimneys that looks like some Disney animator has jammed a hundred small row houses into the vertical... spraying the result with patches of soot, just for shade and accent. Or that's the way it used to look, before the century of smoke was steam-cleaned from its brick exterior and, inside, from its vast glass and arching wrought-iron canopy— repainted, the supporting metal work now revealing decorative curlicues. And looming above it all is the most dominant feature, even distracting from the shops and bakeries and restaurants beyond the tracks, the gently erotic statue of a couple kissing. It's a two-story sculpture, the woman's skirt tight across her bottom, the man's hand not quite touching there but seemingly about to, un-English in the way the station's signature piece should be... Continental and un-insular. Not to mention the normal-sized statue of the portly John Betjeman, poet, journalist and savior of the station. Modern architecture being something of a national challenge in the UK, the wrecking ball is often poised at the wrong times and at the wrong targets.

And that's just the start of the Eurostar experience... for moments after slipping out of London, there's Kent, an otherwise large and green English county that rolls on and on until the North Sea intervenes... but on this Paris-bound train, you miss the whole thing if you stare too long at your coffee. Which, by the way, is not sloshing on your quadriplegic lap, this rail experience being remarkably smooth. These sixty-seven miles of Kent countryside disappear faster than the name: the Channel Tunnel Rail Link. Which was constructed... God only knows how... what with cost overruns and more archaeology than right-of-way. The latter is a fact. Stick a shovel into almost any section of English ground and you come up with history, Roman coins being so common that you would think that Hadrian's army had installed vending machines along the way.

Coming as I do from a country whose infrastructure is crumbling, the soon-to-be-built eleven-mile rail tunnel under

East London seems just as astonishing. City of London banks and financial firms having agreed to a voluntary tax to support much of the construction—these days the very notion of a "voluntary tax" being enough to throw much of America into cardiac arrest. Never mind, and no sense in thinking westward while hurtling eastward. The green blur of Kent stops, of course, when the concrete and fluorescent blur of the Chunnel takes over. Yes, it's not very interesting. Unless you consider this uninteresting thing happening for twenty-two miles, the geological weight of several ice ages and drifting continents resting atop you like a sumo wrestler napping after sex. Which you may or may not be thinking about, the food service being so wonderful aboard Eurostar. A napkin on the lap, a breakfast cappuccino or lunch or dinner wine amplifying the omelet or filet of sole on your plate. And are the French known for fucking around with food?

No wonder you barely notice when the train blasts back into the open air, the free air of free France... all the barbed wire on the Continent side being there to prevent any more immigrants from stealing into Britain, Calais once being infamous for its camp of immigrant detainees. Not that you see any of this, or barely think about it, for the fields of northern France are blasting by. The train hits 186 mph somewhere around here, being 1/100,000th the speed of light, if you want to think about it, which you should. Better, you should think about the turn, the one you can't even see, so gradual it is. But this is required, Paris being slightly south, the train heading east. A ninety-degree turn spread over something like twenty miles. And near the end of the two and one-quarter hours, barely enough time for a decent meal, here come the suburbs of Paris.

Scenic? Or cynic? That is the choice you have. Either marvel at the thing or get all jaded and declare it a bore. Any idea of what this trip used to involve? Rattling out of Victoria Station to Folkstone or Dover, getting off the train and schlepping some distance to a boat. Ferries? I guess that is technically what they are. In the same sense that the English Channel is technically a short sea passage. Actually, it is a watery hell cauldron, periodically smoothed for summer tourists, otherwise bashing away like an apprentice hurricane. A ninety-minute voyage that can seem like days. Followed by another schlep to another train, this one bound for the Gare du Nord... whose platforms will drift into view six hours or so after you said goodbye to London. This happening now aboard Eurostar, six minutes after you said goodbye to your Beaujolais. And even better, there in some strange German Jewish mirror effect, is cousin Bob.

We look vaguely alike, that is the thing... have seen each other through thick and thin since our early twenties... and now, in our sixties, the thick predominates... but we are both still here, that is the other thing. And so are our neuroses, at least mine. Like someone truly filial, I can't help but compare myself to Bob. Early in life, he was a success. A big *macher* in the rarefied world of European economics, a sphere of involvement that has now spread to Asia Minor, the Middle East. And here I am, the wheelchair guy, now retired. And after hugs and a remarkable number of jokes in a small number of minutes... off to my hotel, to which Bob knows the way, having lived here for more than thirty years.

Bob is an action guy, and the Gare du Nord is no place to linger. He's got my bag. I've got a plan. Bob does too, which has to do with the fact that we only see each other every year or two. And it's easy to forget that this is the motorized era of my life, the schlepping era long gone. No, my eighty-kilo wheelchair cannot fit in Bob's Smart Car, although it is just possible that his Smart Car could be carried on my wheelchair.

So... we're fucked, Bendix, is that it, he asks? Actually Bob is indefatigably optimistic. Or so I have always thought. He frowns when I tell him my plan. The Paris transit website shows a wheelchair-accessible bus stop just in front of the station. Bob says he doubts this. Within minutes I doubt it too, for we have just stopped at the transit system's information kiosk, the lovely reception woman hasn't heard of such a thing. I am tired, travel being what it is, but I persevere. Let's ask someone else. Bob throws French around like the airport guys toss baggage. Better, he knows the indigenous politesse, approaching topics like this one with all the correct indirectness. The transit kiosk woman will summon a specialist. A typically French notion, Bob tells me. We prepare to wait. But here he is, the station's assistant manager, slightly rotund, bald and mustachioed like Hercule Poirot. A rapid-fire exchange ensues. No, no, the man tells us, there is no such thing as a bus for wheelchairs. But the transit website? He waves this away. There is, in fact, only one thing to do. Charter a special wheelchair van, the phone number of which he can find, if we would kindly wait just a moment. How much? Seventy-five Euros.

I thank him. Bob thanks him. The cousins must have a discussion now, and we may request his further assistance. Ah, yes, and he is gone. The hotel isn't that far, I tell Bob, it's summertime, and I'm not forking over more than $100 for a van. He can drive my bags to the hotel. We set off, me bouncing toward the Rue La Fayette, Bob in his car. But I don't get far. The blue wheelchair sign on the bus stop in front of the station says everything. The bus that stops there, the driver motioning with his hand that he is about to lower the ramp, says substantially more than anyone in the railway station. Perhaps I am hallucinating this disabled-accessible transit moment. Or perhaps I am a specialist myself, world expert in the maneuverings of the *chaise roulante*. At the hotel Bob seems astonished to see me there so soon. I smile mysteriously.

I have other fish to fry. The hotel was rather vague on the topic of wheelchairs, its website assuring travelers that the management was most sympathetic to disabled travelers. Which translates into a three-inch step into the place, just enough of an obstacle to make my spirits sag. Still, there have been efforts. Someone has beveled the leading edge of the step. And with a spine-jolting run at the thing, my wheelchair can jump it. Which I do, though everyone in the lobby is looking at me. Including Bob. This adds up to a moment of embarrassment, as always, unnecessary.

Which I come to understand soon enough, but first there is the hotel room, reached by one of those bird cage elevators that make one feel so European, not to mention panicked and claustrophobic. Bob takes the stairs, my wheelchair occupying the entire lift, and watches while I try to emerge from it. The narrow hallway demands several back-and-forth maneuvers. The room's narrow doorway requires the same. And inside? Friendly and misguided efforts at wheelchair accessibility. In the toilet, a grab bar oddly placed by the door. The bathtub, a high-rise invention designed for a pole vaulter, does have a grip handle built into the edge. I will be sponge-bathing from the sink. To hell with it, for Paris is outside, Bob rushing back to the office, and I am not going to waste a minute worrying about wheelchair access. For I am hungry.

But actually, hungry for this, the stuff that blossoms as I emerge onto the sidewalk. Arriving, my consciousness was blinkered by fear, the Paris street map gripping my brain and pulling me through intersections, up and down curbs, onward and onward, never mind the glorious and picturesque, such is the eternal vulnerability of the wheelchair traveler. But not now, for Bob will return soon. And the back of The Madeleine is right here. And what is it, this church that looks like the Parthenon? A sign promises concerts. A wedding has just ended. I just have to roll around the place, looking for possible wheelchair entry. Hopeless. I could ask the hotel's concierge, but never mind.

Hungry, I was hungry, so off... and around the block. And damned if life isn't worth it, after all, look at this. I am in Paris, old and crippled and widowed... or is it widowered... and who can say, and who could care? Just look at this neighborhood brasserie, the menu facing the street in a framed lighted holder. For a brief moment I try to convert Euros, then roll away. This restaurant has three front steps. Someone runs in front of me, a guy with a dangling cigarette. I am desperately trying to grasp the simple words he has muttered, shamed by my schoolboy French, which is somewhat irrelevant now. For the real grasp involves this man's hands, not to mention those of his compatriot behind me. I am ascending, like an Indian pasha, turning in midair, as these guys carry me into the restaurant.

I should protest, really I should, but protest what? For this is at the core of disabled travel, maybe life itself. There's no guidebook for this. No map. You just roll down the street and... find that in the middle of this jammed, impersonal, tourist-packed city... people have an idea that we are all in this together. And dinner? I am hardly even alone for this. The guys who carried me in keep coming by and patting me on the shoulder, pouring me more wine. Is this a family-run restaurant or an actual family? And how much wine can I wisely drink, the toilets clearly down a narrow, curving flight of medieval stairs? Never mind, for the hotel is very close, I have had enough, and here's my credit card... and then everything tilts, an earthquake in progress, maybe the wine. No, my airborne exit, the guys unsummoned, smoking and grunting under the staggering weight of steel and lead batteries and me. I thank them profusely, or try to, and they wave lightly and rush back to TV soccer in the bar.

Is it just my wheelchair experience? After all, Americans have this thing about the French, how they are so rude and mean and won't take part in the coalition of the willing, and so on. And everywhere I go, it's the opposite. And by the way, how many American bus drivers, like the French one I encounter the following morning, wear an ironed white shirt and a tie? This one, the young man whose bus is heading in the general direction of the Musée d'Orsay. When we stop along the Seine, just across the river from the museum, he is very concerned. The bridge, he says, may not take wheelchairs.

I am touched, and try to tell him so, rolling from his bus to solid ground. This is the thing about the French, their intense focus on a narrow sphere of endeavor. Which is wonderful in the hands of a man like this one, going to pains to make sure I get off his bus safely. As for the bridge, well, he doesn't know. He isn't in the bridge department. No one else knows, of course. But I do. I don't know how I do, having no information on the Passerelle Solférino. Except what is obvious, that this is a new bridge, constructed in the era of the EU. Rules and regulations and wheelchair access. It is a glorious, single-span design, leading right to the museum. Not only is its slope and general layout quite conducive to wheelchairs, but there is even a nonskid surface. In short, it bridges everything.

END

Lightning Source UK Ltd.
Milton Keynes UK
UKOW032247250612

195052UK00014B/106/P